THE PEARL

A Handbook for Orthodox Converts

DEDICATION

To

THE HOLY ORTHODOX CHURCH

Again the kingdom of heaven is like to a merchant seeking good pearls, who when he found one pearl of great price, went his way, and sold all that he had and bought it. Matthew 13:45-46

THE
PEARL

A Handbook for Orthodox Converts

Michael Whelton

1999

All Scriptural quotations are from the Douay-Rheims version unless otherwise noted.

Regina Orthodox Press
P.O. Box 5288
Salisbury, MA 01952
1-800-636-2470
FAX: 508-462-5079
www.reginaorthodoxpress.com

CONTENTS

ABOUT THE AUTHOR

Michael Whelton is an Orthodox writer whose articles have appeared in various Orthodox magazines and journals. He is also the author of the widely received *Two Paths: Papal Monarchy/Collegial Tradition* in which he examines Rome's claims of papal supremacy in the light of the Orthodox Church.

ACKNOWLEDGEMENTS

To Frank Schaeffer for suggesting both the subject and the title.

INTRODUCTION

Many publishers just publish books, while a few of the more imaginative ones work with their authors by offering suggestions. Frank Schaeffer is certainly one of the latter, since this book owes its existence to him—he suggested both the topic and the title.

When Frank first posed this book, I demurred; however, with some gentle prodding, e.g., "this is your book," I agreed to think it over for a week. During those seven days, the idea began to grow in its appeal and here is the result.

Some books, as they are being written, tend to take on a life and momentum of their own and veer off in a direction not initially intended by the author. *The Pearl* is just such a book. After I completed the first draft, I was left with a nagging feeling that something was missing. There was something else that needed to be said. After some contemplation, it occurred to me to explore the serious challenge of our secular society for the spiritual life of Orthodox Christians (covered in chapters I and X).

Good spiritual literature and a solid understanding of one's faith are absolutely essential. However, it can be detrimental to one's faith if we do not fully understand the secular forces that have created the great spiritual crises of our own age.

For the first time in seventeen hundred years, Western man finds himself in a post-Christian society where with each passing year we witness the steady erosion of Christian influence in our judicial and social life. In the past, Christians lived in a society where all the structures around them reflected and supported their values, e.g., the laws of the land, schools, social mores, etc. This is no longer the case. We now live in a society that is increasingly inimical to Christianity and thus we find ourselves existing as a counterculture.

In order to survive as Orthodox Christians in this environment, we must live our faith more intensely and with a greater awareness of whom we are. It takes heroic virtue to declare that certain things are immoral when our courts of law rule that they are legal, and society is tolerant and even indulgent. Enormous effort is required to instill those values in our children since they are contradicted in the classroom.

In terms of our faith, we could have been born in a much easier time. Yet, God in his wisdom has willed us into existence, to be witnesses of Christ in this age of spiritual crisis. The recognition of this should exhilarate us, since we have been given the challenge to live our Orthodox faith more vigorously and more intensely than in the past. For it is one of the great lessons of history that the Church achieves her most brilliant image when she encounters the abrasive quality of evil manifested in persecution, oppression, and tribulation.

The cosmic victory, of course, is already ours, since the spiritual crises we are witnessing will eventually fade away, as all crises do. There is an old wise saying that warns: "He who marries the spirit of his age is soon a widower." This is a truth readily recognized by American historian Gertrude Himmelfarb when she writes: "It is often said that there is in human beings an irrepressible need for spiritual and moral sustenance. Just as England experienced a resurgence of religion when it seemed most unlikely (the rise of Puritanism in the aftermath of the Renaissance, or of Wesleyanism in the age of deism), so there emerged, at the very height of the Enlightenment, the movement for 'moral reformation.' Today, confronted with an increasingly de-moralized society, we may be ready for a new reformation...."[1]

---

[1] Gertrude Himmelfarb, *The De-Moralization of Society* (New York: Vintage Books, 1996), p. 257.

The Loss of a Christian Vision

Religion blushing veils her sacred fires, and unawares Morality expires. Alexander Pope, *The Dunciad* (1728) 1.649.

Pessimism, which views all change as change for the worse, is, of course, a theme that one sees recurring throughout history with monotonous regularity. However, it is beyond dispute that the predicament of late twentieth-century man differs substantially from that of previous centuries. Much of this is due to the massive loss of faith throughout the Christian West and the subsequent moral vacuum brought about by the loss of moral absolutes.

It is therefore essential that Orthodox Christians understand the secular culture that envelops them and the enormous challenge it poses to their faith. One of the purposes of this book is to address this challenge seriously. Far too many have had their faith swept away by a force which, while felt, was not really understood, i.e., it is one thing to acquire the *Pearl*, it is quite something else to keep it.

CHAPTER I

Someone once made the wise observation that pluralism only appears to exist when society moves from one orthodoxy to another. When the new orthodoxy is firmly in place, the appeal to pluralism is replaced with intolerance for the old order. Christianity has now been shunted to the sidelines by a dominant, secular humanist culture that depreciates and deprecates its values and erodes all its certitudes; e.g., in public schools prayer is now illegal in the U.S. and Canada, and in 1990 all religious celebrations, principally for Christmas, were banned in most Canadian provinces. The exclusion of Christianity from public ceremonies is a growing phenomenon in North America. At the memorial services for the crew of a downed Canadian Forces helicopter crew, the presiding minister "stuck to the generic 'God,' and the Chretien-led 35th Parliament deliberately eliminated references to Christ from the daily Parliamentary prayer."[2]

Abortions are publicly funded and school textbooks now teach that traditional marriage is only one variety among many different family structures. In a British Columbia Supreme Court ruling (December 16, 1998) that ordered the reinstatement of homosexual advocacy books, Justice Mary Saunders explained in her decision that "Freedom of religion includes freedom from religion." The situation in the United States is no

---

[2] *B.C. Report Newsmagazine*, January 11, 1999, p. 60.

different. Let us explore the genesis of this phenomenon.

THE BIRTH OF A RELATIVISTIC AGE

Confusion now hath made his masterpiece! **William Shakespeare,** *Macbeth* **ii.72**

On May 29, 1919, on the tiny, humid, volcanic, malarial island of Principe lying off the equatorial West African coast, Sir Arthur Eddington, director of Cambridge University's observatory, in collaboration with colleagues in Sobral in the Brazilian state of Ceara, took photographs of the total eclipse of the sun. The data he and his colleagues obtained verified Einstein's theory of relativity and exploded the idea that the physical world of time and space could be measured in absolute terms. This discovery swept away a universe ordered on the apparent impregnable thesis of Newtonian physics, "with its straight lines of Euclidean geometry and Galileo's notions of absolute time."[3]

Author Paul Johnson comments that, "in fact, the discovery that space and time are relative rather than absolute terms of measurement is comparable, in its effect on our perception of the

---

[3] Paul Johnson, *Modern Times* (New York: Harper & Row, 1983), p. 1.

world, to the use of perspective in art, which occurred in Greece in the two decades *c.* 500-480 B.C."[4]

The popular culture quickly picked up the idea that since there were no longer any absolutes in the physical world of time and measurement, then this also had to be true for moral absolutes. Thus relativity was invalidly extended to the moral sphere where, "mistakenly but perhaps inevitably, relativity became confused with relativism." Albert Einstein, a highly ethical individual who strenuously upheld an absolute moral code of right and wrong, was appalled.

Absolute truth was now dethroned for the shifting sands of consensus morality, arrived at through opinion polls; e.g., 62% of people believe that abortion, pre-marital sex, assisted suicide, etc., are acceptable, therefore....

CONSCIENCE DETHRONED

Conscience and grace, to the profoundest pit!
I dare damnation. William Shakespeare, *Hamlet* v. 130

The public response to relativity was one of the principal formative influences on the course of

---

[4] Ibid., p. 1.

twentieth-century history. "It formed a knife, inadvertently wielded by its author, to help cut society adrift from its traditional moorings in the faith and morals of Judeo-Christian culture."[5]

Author Paul Johnson explores the highly combustible effect of relativity when mixed with the almost simultaneous public reception of the writings of Sigmund Freud, in whose analysis "the personal conscience, which stood at the very heart of the Judeo-Christian ethic, and was the principal engine of individualistic achievement, was dismissed as a mere safety-device, collectively created, to protect civilized order from the fearful aggressiveness of human beings."[6]

In fact, Freud contended that the repression of desire demanded by mature societies placed human happiness beyond reach. "His revelation of the power of sexual urges and the unconscious mind reduced confidence in the moral will." Freud's teaching in psychoanalysis "undermined the orthodox belief of Western man, established since Greek times, in the priority of reason."[7]

The impact of Einstein's relativity and Freud's psychoanalysis on the artistic and intellectual

---

[5] Ibid., p. 5.
[6] Ibid., p. 11.
[7] C. B. Cox and A. E. Dyson (eds.), *The Twentieth Century Mind* (Oxford University Press, 1972), vol. 2, p. x.

CHAPTER I

community was quick and immense. In 1919 the French writer Marcel Proust published the first volume of his novel *Remembrance of Things Past,* a work Johnson describes as "a vast experiment in disjointed time and subterranean sexual emotions which epitomized the new preoccupations."[8] The expatriate Irishman James Joyce published his book *Ulysses* in Paris in 1922. This work was so controversial that only a small private press could print it. With countries such as Britain and the United States banning it as obscene, the novel had to be smuggled like contraband across many frontiers. However, as Paul Johnson comments, "its significance was not missed. No novel illustrated more clearly the extent to which Freud's concepts had passed into the language of literature."[9]

The great American-born British poet and critic T. S. Eliot claimed that Proust and Joyce had "destroyed the whole nineteenth century"--an age whose literature celebrated the Christian virtues of personal responsibility and accountability, and whose authors displayed a genuine concern for the impact their works had on the morals of their readers. Today modern society would derisively call such works "moralistic." *Remembrance of Things Past* and *Ulysses* heralded the moving away from the spiritual and moral values of the

---

[8] Johnson, *Modern Times,* p. 9.
[9] Ibid., p. 9.

THE LOSS OF A CHRISTIAN VISION

Christian West. The result marked "not merely the entrance of the anti-hero but the destruction of individual heroism as a central element in imaginative creation, and a contemptuous lack of concern for moral balance-striking and verdicts. The exercise of individual free will ceased to be the supremely interesting feature of human behavior."[10] Today we find writers expressing the spirit of their age in images of isolation--the outsider, the refugee, the alien, the exile.

The impact of relativity, or more accurately relativism, found fertile soil in the predominantly Protestant western society, especially in North America, with its anti-hierarchical egalitarian principle.

THE PROTESTANT EXPERIENCE

All protestantism, even the most cold and passive, is a sort of dissent. But the religion most prevalent in our northern colonies is a refinement on the principle of resistance; it is the dissidence of dissent, and the protestantism of the Protestant religion. Edmund Burke [1722-1797], *Speech on Conciliation with America*

The shattering of Western Christianity that began with the Protestant Revolt over four hundred

---

[10] Johnson, *Modern Times,* p. 10.

CHAPTER I

years ago continues to this day. While the countless varieties of different denominations almost defy definition, there is still one doctrine they hold in common –*Sola Scriptura* (by scripture alone). This doctrine affirms the supremacy of individuals in their private interpretation of Scripture and is the very seminal seed of Protestantism. For with this, every believer becomes his own sovereign pontiff.

In his book *Dancing Alone*, novelist and film director Frank Schaeffer relates his personal journey from Protestantism to the Orthodox Church and records the damage wreaked by private judgment and its ensuing pluralism within this religious body:

> No bishop, apostolic or otherwise, had any special authority over us regarding the true meaning of Scripture. No Father of the Church or Council had any special wisdom to which we should hearken. In fact, we were told that our Christianity was like the rest of life in our pluralistic, free society--up to the individual, a personal choice, a question of individual "leading." Our Christianity was, in fact, anything we wanted it to be, though perhaps we never admitted as much. We said that what we believed was biblical. But it often turned out that the Bible said anything we wanted it to. We tended to reject the ancient Christian idea that the Holy Spirit had led the Church. Yet we readily enough claimed the Spirit's "leading," on a personal

THE LOSS OF A CHRISTIAN VISION

subjective level, as proof that we were correct about matters theological and "doing the Lord's Will" in matters personal. If we disagreed with the teaching of one denomination or minister, we would shop for a new "church" until we found one we liked.[11]

The doctrine of *Sola Scriptura* is like a faulty gene embedded in the genetic code of Protestantism that causes it to perpetually mutate, thus guaranteeing to deny it doctrinal cohesion. It is therefore condemned to do what it has always done, divide, sub-divide and divide again. There are now thousands of different denominations with competing theologies—and new ones cropping up every year. Thus, while Protestantism failed to give North American society a cohesive doctrinal presence as an antidote to secular humanism, it rather aided it. As Schaeffer observes, "...since all religious ideas are equally true, even when they contradict each other, then they must be equally irrelevant to public life and serve no purpose beyond private individual therapeutic needs."[12] Truth relativism, that is so fundamental to pluralism, found major unwitting support in Protestant doctrine. From the primacy of private judgment flows the anti-hierarchical principle and its fellow traveler–egalitarianism.

---

[11] Frank Schaeffer, *Dancing Alone* (Brookline, Massachusetts: Holy Cross Orthodox Press, 1994), pp. 1-2.
[12] Ibid., p. 3.

CHAPTER I

For Christian civilization, belief in God involved the acceptance of moral absolutes that governed human behavior, which in turn elevated aesthetic standards to conform to this ideal. This idealistic foundation expressed our vision of supreme excellence and, in the past, any human being that came close to embodying these qualities was worthy of emulation. In fact, the classical world took this a step further and regarded the highest as the norm and anything below it as a corruption. They pursued this ideal of perfection in all facets of human experience—justice, reason, physical beauty—and attempted to hold all in harmony and equilibrium. Christianity readily fused this Greek ideal with its own system of thought to give Christian civilization its philosophical and artistic creative power—its genius.

Egalitarianism attacks this idealistic foundation on which Christianity rests by preaching a uniformity that cannot peacefully coexist with a concept of excellence and perfection. As British professor Duncan Williams observes in his book, *The Trousered Apes,* egalitarianism in its pursuit of uniformity induces a state of nervous timidity when it comes to upholding normative standards of behavior, which leads to "an uncritical acceptance of relativism. Ultimately all actions and values and vice, normalcy and abnormality, truth and falsehood, become meaningless and social; aesthetic and cultural anarchy prevails. The result

THE LOSS OF A CHRISTIAN VISION

is a society in which everything is permitted—the final triumph of egalitarianism since all human actions (as well as men) are reduced to a state of unjudgeable equality."[13]

A MORAL TWILIGHT

> For the heart of this people is grown gross, and with their ears have they heard heavily, and their eyes have they shut; lest perhaps they should see with their eyes, and hear with their ears and understand with their heart, and should be converted, and I should heal them. Acts 28:24-27

The scandal surrounding U.S. President Bill Clinton provided a glaring example of a nation plunged into a moral vacuum by its unwillingness to pass judgment on its president. For in spite of his adultery, blatant lying to the public, perjury, and obstruction of justice, Bill Clinton's popularity remained undiminished. It is in this moral twilight that the United States Senate refused to impeach the president. In refusing to pass judgment on Bill Clinton, the senators passed judgment on themselves for heaping dishonor on the country they swore to serve and for eroding its judiciary.

---

[13] Duncan Williams, *Trousered Apes* (New Rochelle, NY: Arlington House, 1972), p. 100.

CHAPTER I

Ian Hunter, a professor of law, bemoans the effect this sordid state of affairs has on the moral and judicial environment in his book, *Three Faces of the Law*:

> The ultimate danger, and in my opinion this danger is upon us, is that we lose the faculty of judging, the capacity to discriminate between good and evil, innocence and guilt. And with it we lose the moral authority to punish transgressors.

> Let there be no mistake: at the end of this road is not tolerance but tyranny. When we shrug off the, perhaps now wearisome, burden of judging, we shall not find a utopia, a tolerant city set upon a hill; we shall find a concentration camp.[14]

Author William J. Bennett comments:

> How do we judge a wrong--any wrong whatsoever-- when we have gutted the principle of judgment itself? What arguments can be made after we have strip-mined all the arguments of their force, their power, and their ability to inspire public outrage? We all know that there are times when we will have to judge others when it is both right and *necessary* to judge others. If we do not confront the soft relativism that is currently disguised as a virtue, we

---

[14] Ian Hunter, *Three Faces of the Law* (Mississauga, Ontario: Work Research Foundation, 1996), p. 27.

will find ourselves morally and intellectually disarmed. [15]

Egalitarianism was able to destroy normative standards of behavior by society's unconscious substitution of "values" for virtues. As American historian Gertrude Himmelfarb shows in her book *The De-Moralization of Society,* "values reduce morality to the level of mere customs and social conventions." When morality was anchored to the word "virtue," it possessed "a firm and resolute character...a sense of gravity and authority, as 'values' does not."[16] She comments further:

Values, as we now understand that word, do not have to be virtues; they can be beliefs, opinions, attitudes, feelings, habits, conventions, preferences, prejudices, even idiosyncrasies—whatever any individual, group, or society happens to value, at any time, for any reason. One cannot say of virtues, as one can say of values, that anyone's virtues are as good as anyone else's, or that everyone has a right to his own virtues. Only values can lay that claim to moral equality and neutrality. This impartial, 'nonjudgmental,' as we now say, sense of values—values as 'value free'—is now so firmly

---

[15] *Imprimis*, 27, no. 12, December 1998 (Hillsdale, Michigan: Hillsdale College).
[16] Gertrude Himmelfarb, *The De-Moralizing of Society* (New York: Vintage Books, 1996), p. 11.

CHAPTER I

entrenched in the popular vocabulary and sensibility that one can hardly imagine a time without it.[17]

The substitution of values for virtues, in reducing morality to mere customs and social conventions, was to provide an environment where laws are created to gratify "maximum choice in the pursuit of personal fulfillment, subject only to constraints where conduct might lead to unhappiness for others; thus in our own society the law has been amended to decriminalize abortion and homosexual practices between consenting adults, and to abolish impediments to personal self-expression as the censorship of literature or the theatre."[18]

The irony is, of course, that while all conservative Protestants strenuously uphold virtue, it is the "truth relativism" inherent in Protestantism that undermines it.

The contemporary Protestant religious experience runs the gamut from the traditional, conservative Southern Baptists to the likes of New York's Episcopal Bishop Spong, who in 1989 ordained to the priesthood a professed homosexual in the "fervent hope that his life could offer to the homosexual population of our metropolitan area a model of holiness, fidelity and

---

[17] Ibid., pp. 11-12

[18] Anne Glyn-Jones, *Holding Up A Mirror* (London: Century Books, 1996), pp. 8-9.

monogamy with which we could counter promiscuity and other forms of predatory or casual sexual behavior."[19] It was not so long ago that, if one had dreamed up such a situation, one would have been guilty of very bad taste.

In Canada's largest Protestant body, The United Church of Canada, "there are 27 openly lesbian and gay clergy, 'at least 200' more are still in the closet. Nine congregations have completed the 'Affirming Congregation' process of fully welcoming homosexuals in their midst."[20] The head of the United Church of Canada, Rev. Bill Phipps, has informed the public that he no longer believes in the divinity of Jesus.[21] All the numerous Protestant denominations have substantially moved away from the creeds and confessions of their 16th century founders. The dynamics of personal autonomy and private judgment, while offering no defense against secular humanism, is also causing grievous self-inflicted damage to some of the mainline churches, as we have just seen. In fact, it would be an act of honesty if these churches dispensed with the name "Christian," since they have so obviously abdicated the substance.

---

[19] *Church Times*, February 9, 1990.
[20] *B.C. Report*, October 19, 1998, p. 59.
[21] Ibid.

CHAPTER I

In his book, *A House Divided: Protestantism, Schism and Secularization*, author Steven Bruce observes that "...the fragmentation produced by Protestantism was central in that a monolithic religious culture would have provided greater resistance to secularization."[22] For a while, it looked as if the Roman Catholic Church were capable of providing that necessary resistance, as we shall see next.

THE ROMAN CATHOLIC CHURCH

How doth the city sit solitary that was once full of people! How is the mistress of the gentiles become as a widow: ...there is none to comfort her among all them that were dear to her: all her friends have despised her, and are become her enemies....all her gates are broken down: her priests sigh: her virgins are in affliction, and she is oppressed with bitterness...And from the daughter of Sion all her beauty is departed.[23]

With these verses from the *Lamentations of Jeremiah*, Canadian author Anne Roche Muggeridge begins her book, *The Desolate City,* in which, with intense sadness, she records "the complete and rapid collapse of the Catholic world"

---

[22] Steven Bruce, *A House Divided: Protestantism, Schism and Secularization* (New York: Routledge, 1990), p. 27.

[23] Anne Roche Muggeridge, *The Desolate City* (Toronto, Canada: McClelland and Stewart, 1986), p. 7.

she grew up in. "For Catholicism is today like a city ravaged by war. The spires have fallen, the wells are poisoned, the government is in exile. Those citizens who cannot bear to flee wander sadly through the ruins, trying to salvage objects not too damaged to be useful. Families are divided, neighbors turned cold."[24]

One of the most surprising developments of this century has been the catastrophic decline of the powerful Roman Catholic Church, the speed of which can only be described as breathtaking. Prior to the Second Vatican Council (1962-1965), this powerful, enormously confident church looked absolutely unassailable. In fact, the decades leading up to the Second Vatican Council were a golden age for North American Catholicism, with the much revered, austere Pope Pius XII presiding over legions of disciplined priests and nuns and an obedient loyal laity. For a while, this citadel of certitude, rising out of a sea of Protestant chaos, looked as if it would be the moral conscience of society. Then came the Second Vatican Council and, as Clifford Geertz once observed, "nothing alters quite like the unalterable."[25]

---

[24] Ibid.

[25] Michael W. Cuneo, *The Smoke of Satan: Conservative and Traditionalist Dissent in Contemporary American Catholicism* (New York: Oxford University Press, 1997), p. 14.

CHAPTER I

The damage most immediately felt, following the Council, was to its priesthood, as ordinations and vocations went into a steep and protracted decline accompanied by wholesale defections. Ironically, it was the priesthood that initially displayed the most enthusiasm for the Council. As Fordham University's Michael W. Cuneo observes in his book *The Smoke of Satan:*

> By according positive religious significance to worldly affairs—by sanctifying, in a way, the secular order—the council implicitly raised doubts concerning the purpose and value of an expressly religious vocation....If only indirectly, however, the council removed much of this luster from the religious vocation. If the secular world is alive with redemptive possibility and, as the council also taught, political and scientific activity is a conveyance of faith, what is then the point of subjecting oneself to the rigors of asceticism?[26]

The rise of militant feminism, accompanied by an unrelenting assault on all forms of traditional authority in the years following the Council, only further weakened the vocational commitment in Catholic religious life. "The catch phrase of the day was 'personal autonomy,' and within this broader context the discipline and docility of religious life came to seem positively freakish."[27]

---

[26] Ibid., p. 16.
[27] Ibid.

Then it was the turn of the laity, with the destruction of the ancient Mass of the Roman Rite, much of which dates from the 6th century, a situation Rome's foremost liturgical scholar, Monsignor Klaus Gamber, described as "a liturgical destruction of startling proportions...a debacle worsening with each passing year."[28] Churches were stripped of much of their statuary; magnificent altars were ripped out of the sanctuaries and replaced with bare tables. Sacred altar furnishings, e.g., old chalices, monstrances, etc., ended up in pawnshops and antique shops. Tabernacles and monstrances form part of the décor at several Toronto restaurants.[29] A long period of liturgical anarchy followed, with the more extreme form featuring priests in psychedelic vestments and clown masses.

As I mentioned in my book *Two Paths,* "Most Roman Catholics do not read Papal Encyclicals or Papal Addresses; the Church speaks to her faithful as she always has, through the liturgy."[30] What was being communicated now was that the "unalterable" had indeed been altered. The timeless *Mass of the Roman Rite* had been replaced with a liturgy drained of mysticism and

[28] Monsignor Klaus Gamber , *The Reform of the Roman Liturgy* (San Juan Capistrano, California: Una Voce Press, and Harrison, New York: Foundation for Catholic Reform, 1993), p. 9.
[29] Roche Muggeridge, p. 130.
[30] Michael Whelton, *Two Paths* (Salisbury, Massachusetts: Regina Orthodox Press, 1998), p. 10.

drama. For the Catholic laity, the center of their spiritual lives had changed beyond recognition, and Mass attendance went into a steep decline from which it has never recovered.

It is now thirty-four years since the closing of the Council; the Roman Catholic Church remains a shadow of her former self, as the following sad statistics clearly show for the Church in the United States:

Seminarians

	1965:	48,992
	1995:	5,083

Priests

	1965:	58,632
	1995:	49,551

Brothers teaching

	1965:	5,868
	1995:	1,564

Brothers

	1965:	12,271
	1995:	6,578

Sisters

	1965:	179,954
	1995:	92,107

THE LOSS OF A CHRISTIAN VISION

High school students,
Diocesan and parish
        1965: 698,032
        1995: 378,847[31]

An even bleaker picture for the priesthood is revealed when we learn that "by the turn of the century, or shortly thereafter, almost half of all active priests will be age fifty-five or older, and only 10 percent or so will be age thirty-five or younger."[32] Priestless parishes will be a common feature of the future Roman Catholic landscape. Also since the Council, the laity have absorbed further liturgical innovations such as lay people distributing communion, altar girls, and liturgical dance. They wait with a nervous, hesitant curiosity as to what will come next.

Nevertheless, Catholics have joined their Protestant brethren in "privatizing religion", i.e., selecting and rejecting doctrines based on need and personal preferences; e.g., many reject church teaching on abortion, artificial contraception, homosexuality, and the ordination of women.[33]

---

[31] Kenneth Jones, "Three Decades of Renewal," *The Latin Mass* (Winter 1996), 32-35, compiled from the Official Catholic Directory of 1965 and 1995.

[32] Michael Cuneo, p. 15.

[33] Adrian Hastings (ed.), *Modern Catholicism: Vatican II and After* (New York: Oxford University Press, 1991), p. 331.

CHAPTER I

However, within this chaotic scene of late twentieth century society, there are increasing numbers of Protestants and Roman Catholics who are leaving their compromised communions and entering the doors of the Orthodox Church. For she alone has preserved and proclaimed the original Christian faith undiluted, with nothing added to or taken away since the time of the Apostles--a splendid enduring witness to Christian tradition.

THE QUEST

Instead of asking if Christian forebears like Anselm, Augustine, Athanasius, and Chrysostom were in our Church, we began to ask if we were in theirs![34]

The Orthodox Church in North America, a once placid, retiring, cultural curiosity, is displaying astonishing strength and vitality. Metropolitan Philip Saliba once called the Orthodox Church "the best kept secret in America"; however, this may no longer be the case, since the *Encyclopaedia Britannica Year Book for 1995 and 1996* lists the Orthodox Church as the fastest growing mainline church in North America. "At St. Vladimir's Orthodox Seminary in New York, 50 percent of the students are from non-Orthodox backgrounds. In the Orthodox Church in America about half of the

---

[34] Peter E. Gillquist, *Becoming Orthodox* (Ben Lomond, California: Conciliar Press, 1992), p. 185.

THE LOSS OF A CHRISTIAN VISION

bishops are from non-Orthodox backgrounds."[35] When I share this piece of information with cradle Orthodox Christians here in Canada, I am always met with wide-eyed looks of incredulity.

To many people, the Orthodox Church looks like "Roman Catholicism without the Pope"; however, on closer inspection it turns out to be "something quite distinct from any religious system in the west. Yet those who look more closely at this 'unknown world' will discover much in it which, while different, is yet curiously familiar. 'But that is what I have always believed!'"[36] Converts to the Orthodox Church follow many different paths: some are easy while many are difficult; however, armed with a burning love for the truth they press on. For the reward is incomparable--a tremendous spiritual peace, a joyous homecoming to the Church of the Apostles and Martyrs. The common thread that runs through many of the conversion stories is a search for the New Testament Church in the historical record.

A collective gasp could be heard from the Protestant community when Frank Schaeffer, the son of the late Francis Schaeffer, one of this century's most prominent evangelical theologians,

---

[35] Daniel B. Clendenin, *Eastern Orthodox Christianity: A Western Perspective* (Grand Rapids, Michigan: Baker Books, 1994), p. 12.
[36] Timothy Ware, *The Orthodox Church* (London, England: Penguin Books, 1973), p. 10.

35

CHAPTER I

was received into the Orthodox Church. His spiritual journey is eloquently told in his book *Dancing Alone,*[37] which includes a withering analysis and indictment of the state of religion in North America. Schaeffer's spiritual journey began "when," he writes, "I started to ask questions about what seemed to me to be the evident spiritual bankruptcy of Protestantism and the intensely secularized pluralistic culture it had produced.... I began to read the Church Fathers and study Church history.... A day came when it became clear to me that if I was to believe the history books I was reading and the writings of the Fathers of the Church, then I had to choose between the Protestant world view and the Holy Tradition. What was obvious was that they were not one and the same."[38] In addition to being a film director, novelist, and much sought-after speaker, Frank Schaeffer also operates a successful Orthodox publishing house.

One of the more recent luminaries to enter the Orthodox Church was the prominent American historian, Jaroslav Pelikan. Pelikan was born in the United States on December 17, 1923, to highly cultured Czech immigrant parents, where even as a young boy he was "very conscious of Europe and

---

[37] See footnote, p. 21.
[38] Schaeffer, p. xviii.

36

European ways."[39] Major avenues of transmission for this culture were the languages he learnt from his parents, i.e., Slovak, Serbian, Czech, and German. Both his father and paternal grandfather were Lutheran ministers; thus Pelican describes the atmosphere in his home as one "where both the theological tradition and humanistic culture were so much my daily bread that I still find the present antithesis between them quite incomprehensible."[40]

After being nurtured in such a rich intellectual environment, it is little wonder that Jaroslav Pelikan went on to pursue an illustrious academic career. In 1972, he was awarded the Sterling chair of history in the Graduate School of Arts and Sciences at Yale University. He received the prestigious Cross Medal of the Yale Graduate School Association in 1979 and in 1984 he was elected to give the William Clyde DeVane Lectures. Since the beginning of his tenure at Yale University in 1962, Pelikan's written output has been prodigious, having written or edited over twenty-five books and over a hundred articles and essays.

---

[39] M. Bauman and M. I. Klauber, *Historians of the Christian Division, Their Methodology and Influence on Western Thought* (Nashville, Tennessee: Broadman & Holman Publishers, 1995), p. 551.

[40] Ibid., p. 552.

CHAPTER I

It is for his outstanding scholarship and output that more than thirty-four colleges and universities have awarded him an honorary doctorate. The National Endowment for the Humanities honored Jaroslav Pelikan by selecting him as a Senior Fellow in 1967-68, and in 1983 bestowed its highest honor on him when he was asked to deliver the Jefferson Lecture in the Humanities.

As a Christian historian, Pelikan has striven to give recognition to the major contribution of Eastern Christendom—a contribution long overlooked by the West. As Pelikan himself observes, "'The liturgical, political, and doctrinal history of Eastern Christendom is an indispensable component of any responsible research in [the history of Christianity], but ignoring the Christian East has long been characteristic both of the churchmanship and of the scholarship of the West, whether Roman Catholic or Protestant.' In addition to many details and nuances woven into his writings, Pelikan's inclusion of this 'indispensable component' is evident in both the amount of attention he gives to and the sensitivity he demonstrates toward Eastern Christianity."[41]

This great scholar entered the Orthodox Church at St. Vladimir's Seminary in Crestwood, New York, in 1998.

---

[41] Ibid., p. 556.

THE LOSS OF A CHRISTIAN VISION

A long spiritual journey to the New Testament Church made by 2000 evangelical Protestants culminated in 1987, when, over a period of two months, seventeen parishes from Nashville, Tennessee, to Anchorage, Alaska, embraced the Orthodox faith. This remarkable spiritual journey is movingly related in Fr. Peter Gillquist's book, *Becoming Orthodox.*[42] During the 1960's, Peter Gillquist was the Northern Regional Director of the Campus Crusade for Christ. Today Father Peter Gillquist is chairman of the Department of Missions and Evangelism for the Antiochian Orthodox Christian Archdiocese of North America. Since 1987, his department has brought sixty congregations into the Orthodox Church.

---

[42] Peter Gillquist, *Becoming Orthodox: A Journey to the Ancient Christian Faith* (Ben Lomond, California: Conciliar Press, 1992).

The Church of the Apostles and Martyrs

For me the initial delight is in the surprise of remembering something I didn't know I knew. There is a glad recognition of the long lost....
Robert Frost

The first time my wife and I entered an Orthodox Church was in southern Greece. It was a picturesque little town of dazzling white homes with window boxes spilling over with red geraniums and a peacock blue sea stretching in the distance. We entered the little basilica-style church and were greeted with a lingering fragrance of incense and a myriad of colorful icons and murals of ancient saints gazing from the shadowy walls. Together with the beautiful iconostasis, gold altar furnishings and numerous standing candelabra with their flickering candles, it was an incredible scene of visual richness. We couldn't help contrasting this scene with the Frank Lloyd Wright glass and cedar churches at home, with their Calvinistic astringency of bare walls and potted plants.

Here was a more ancient, sensual, mystical Christianity that had no misgivings about

41

CHAPTER II

communicating the world of the sacred through the medium of the senses, e.g., the visual aesthetic beauty and the wonderful fragrance of incense. As we stood in this church we felt a vague, almost indefinable impression of something authentic—an intuitive recognition of a truth. The words of John Keats immediately came to mind: "I can never feel certain of any truth but from a clear perception of its beauty."[43] Here in the silence of this little Orthodox Church came the "surprise of remembering something we didn't know we knew." For in contrast to our own aesthetically barren, post-Vatican II churches, with their "kindergarten" felt banners hanging in and around the sanctuaries, the spiritual world was presented to us in a lavish, unself-conscious display of beauty reflecting the glory of God's creation.

The surprise of remembering the importance of aesthetic beauty in our religious life was something we took home with us. As a result of this encounter, we developed an interest in the Orthodox Church and her art. Many years later, after much study and soul searching, we embraced the Orthodox Church, but one of the catalysts and precipitating causes was her beauty and the "glad recognition of the long lost."

---

[43] To George and Georgiana Keats, 16 Dec. 1818 – 4 Jan. 1819.

THE CHURCH OF THE APOSTLES AND MARTYRS

A ZEALOUS GUARDIAN OF TRADITION

Therefore, brethren, stand fast; and hold the traditions which you have learned, whether by word, or by our epistle. 2 Thess. 2:14

For at least the first thousand years Christendom was an undivided church governed by councils "that offered a common forum for both churches east and west to settle differences and thus provide a common bond."[44] It is provable beyond doubt that "the Early Church does not point to the office of a single bishop as the living tradition of the Church, but to an ecumenical consensus or collective conscience, which is best exemplified by the early general councils. It is this model of government that is intrinsic to the nature of the Church and it is this that supplies her with enduring strength and stability."[45]

Today the Orthodox Church is the only church in Christendom that preserves and guards this collegial tradition; thus she rightly calls herself *The Church of the Seven Ecumenical Councils,* those giant pillars of the faith. Today with her self-governing churches bound together in a fraternal unity, she presents herself to the world just as the

---

[44] Whelton, p. 103.
[45] Ibid., p. 200.

43

CHAPTER II

Early Church did. As Bishop Kallistos Ware observes:

> The Orthodox Church is thus a family of self-governing Churches. It is held together, not by a centralized organization, not by a single prelate wielding absolute power over the whole body, but by the double bond of unity in the faith and communion in the sacraments. Each Church, while independent, is in full agreement with the rest on all matters of doctrine, and between them all there is full sacramental communion.[46]

As a zealous guardian of Apostolic Tradition, the Orthodox Church is able to present the full deposit of faith to those increasing numbers of spiritually hungry souls who come to her doorstep seeking admittance. As their natural mother, she lovingly welcomes them home.

The greatest tragedy to befall Christendom was the division between the Latin West and Orthodox-Byzantine East. The date popularly given for this schism is 1054 when papal legates and Michael Cerularius, the Patriarch of Constantinople, excommunicated each other. "A more sure date for the final separation between the two great churches would be April 12, 1204, when the 4th Crusade attacked and sacked Constantinople for 30 days, which Sir Steven Runciman describes as

---

[46] Ware, p. 15.

THE CHURCH OF THE APOSTLES AND
MARTYRS

'one of the most ghastly and tragic incidents in history....'"[47] Rome then imposed a Latin Patriarch of Constantinople on the Orthodox population, which continued until 1261 when the Byzantines recaptured the city. This monstrous act committed by fellow Christians was a source of revulsion and bitterness for the Orthodox. This coupled with the newfound claims of a vigorous, papal monarchy created a wide chasm.

Because SS. Peter and Paul were martyred in Rome and because Rome was the ancient seat of government, Rome enjoyed a certain pre-eminence, a primacy of honor—first among equals (primus inter pares) among her sister Patriarchates, i.e., Constantinople, Alexandria, Antioch, and Jerusalem. The Orthodox Church believes that Rome erred in attempting to turn this "primacy of honor" within the Church to a supremacy over the Church.

Two radically different models of church government accentuated this tragic, widening chasm between Rome and the Orthodox world. With four of the five Patriarchal sees in the East, i.e., Constantinople, Alexandria, Antioch and Jerusalem, the Orthodox Church was able to preserve the conciliar nature of the Church that one finds reflected in the Council of Jerusalem and

---

[47] Whelton, p. 94.

the Seven Ecumenical Councils. In the early Church the ecumenical councils represented the highest judicial body. These councils were not called to advise the Bishop of Rome, and the Bishop of Rome did not enjoy veto power. Nowhere in the canons or creeds do we find any recognition of Rome's claim to supreme universal jurisdiction. None of the Church Fathers or General Councils settled doctrinal disputes by appealing to an infallible pope. Claims of infallibility by a single bishop would have been incomprehensible. Furthermore, the idea that the Bishop of Rome was superior to a council of the Church and that a council was only ecumenical because the Bishop of Rome alone confirmed its decrees was unknown. In fact, all five Patriarchates, Rome, Constantinople, Alexandria, Antioch, and Jerusalem, had to confirm the decrees. The Church of the Seven Ecumenical Councils called for an equilibrium that we find in Canon 34 of the Apostolic Canons. These canons date from the first half of the fourth century and mirror the practices of the pre-Nicaean Church. These canons were translated into Latin by Dionysius Exiguus in the late 5th century and were widely accepted in the West. Canon 34 reads as follows:

> The bishops of every nation must acknowledge him who is first among them and account him as their head and do nothing of consequence without his consent; but each may do those things which

concern his own parish and the country places which belong to it. But neither let him who is the first do anything without the consent of all. For so there will be oneness of mind and God will be glorified through the Lord in the Holy Spirit.[48]

Thus it was crystal clear that no bishop could claim supreme universal jurisdiction since he could do nothing *without the consent of all.* In 419 the bishops of North Africa informed Pope Celestine that "all matters should be terminated in the places where they arise" and that they "did not think that the grace of the Holy Spirit would be wanting to any Province." No single bishop can place himself above a council "unless it be imagined that God can inspire a single individual with justice, and refuse it to an innumerable multitude of bishops assembled in council."[49]

St. Cyprian reminds us of this essential equality of all bishops in his celebrated dispute with Pope St. Stephen over the issue of heretical baptism. Since this is such a key issue dividing the two great churches of Christendom, I have presented

---

[48] John Meyendorff, *Byzantine Theology* (Scarsdale, New York: St. Vladimir's Seminary Press, 1974), p. 80.

[49] *The Seven Ecumenical Councils of the Undivided Church: Their Canons and Dogmatic Decrees,* in *Nicene and Post-Nicene Fathers,* 2nd series, vol. 14 (Peabody, Mass.: Hendrickson, 1994), p. 510. As quoted in John Meyendorff, *Catholicity and the Church* (Crestwood, New York: St. Vladimir's Seminary Press, 1979), p. 114.

CHAPTER II

this subject in some detail. This famous
controversy provides a stunning affirmation to the
claim of the Orthodox Church that the Church was
always collegial in its government, as opposed to
Rome's view, in that her supreme universal
jurisdiction is "the venerable and constant belief of
every age" recognized "always and everywhere
and by all."[50]

This famous controversy is chronicled as
follows:

ST. CYPRIAN OF CARTHAGE
BISHOP AND MARTYR (C 200-258)

**For no one of us setteth himself as a Bishop of bishops,
or by tyrannical terror forceth his colleagues to a
necessity of obeying; inasmuch as every bishop, in the
free use of his liberty and power, has the right of
forming his own judgment, and can no more be judged
by another than he can himself judge another. St.
Cyprian.[51]**

Carthage, one of the most famous cities of the
ancient world, was founded by the Phoenicians in
the eighth century, and Hannibal, its famous son,
dared to challenge the might of Rome. After
Hannibal's defeat, the Romans razed the city to the

---

[50] Pope Leo XIII, *Satis Cognitum.*
[51] Mansi, I, 951

ground and to ensure its barrenness covered the land with salt.

Eventually, the Romans returned and built a new dazzling city of great buildings, theatres, villas, and baths. This new Carthage became the administrative capital of Africa; its importance can be measured by the size of its Antonine thermal baths. The size of a city's baths are usually a good gauge as to the importance Romans attributed to a city; judging from the size of these baths, Carthage obviously enjoyed a high degree of prestige, for the dimensions of the Antonine thermal baths make it one of the greatest ever built in the Roman Empire—the "cool room" alone is a colossal 154 feet long and 49 feet high. The annual summer festival of Carthage is held in the original Roman theatre.

From the second century on, the city had its own bishop--the most famous one being St. Cyprian. Today ancient Carthage is a suburb of the city of Tunis on Tunisia's Mediterranean coast, with wild flowers growing among its sun-baked ruins.

St. Cyprian was born into a noble pagan family in Carthage in the first decade of the third century and received an excellent education in literature and rhetoric. As a result of his great gifts as a rhetorician, he was able to move with ease among the ranks of high society, gaining many influential friends in the process. St. Cyprian came to Christianity late in life in the year 246 when he was in his forties. Due to his high reputation, he was elected bishop of Carthage two years later in 248. He suffered martyrdom by beheading ten years afterwards on September 14, 258, uttering only the words "Deo Gratias" (thanks be to God) upon hearing his sentence.

St. Cyprian is perhaps best known for his long-standing dispute with Pope Stephen over the rebaptizing of heretics, and it is this famous confrontation that provides considerable insight into the understanding of Church authority in the 3rd century.

Persecutions of Christians in the Roman Empire had always been a sporadic and local phenomenon; however, this was to change shortly after St. Cyprian's consecration as Bishop of Carthage. In January, 250, the Roman Emperor Decius issued an imperial edict ordering all citizens to sacrifice to the Roman gods in the presence of government commissioners who then issued a certificate (*libellus*) as proof of their sacrifice. An automatic death sentence awaited those who refused. The Decian persecution was the first organized attempt to stamp out Christianity in the Roman Empire; it was to end in failure, with the majority of Christians, including the bishops of

THE CHURCH OF THE APOSTLES AND MARTYRS

Rome, Jerusalem, and Antioch, choosing martyrdom.

Peace returned in 251 to a divided and troubled Church. In Rome two competing factions had elected rival candidates in the persons of Cornelius and Novatian for the empty see (St. Cyprian recognized Cornelius). The great challenge facing the Church was how to deal with the lapsed, i.e., those Christians who had sacrificed to the Roman gods. St. Cyprian counseled charity and, to insure uniformity of treatment, the African bishops convened a council and adopted a common policy towards the lapsed, informing Rome of their decision "lest our numbers should not seem enough."[52] It was to this troubled and divided Church that St. Cyprian wrote his impassioned treatise *On the Unity of the Catholic Church*:

> And this unity we ought firmly to hold and assert, especially those of us that are bishops who preside in the Church, that we may also prove the episcopate itself to be one and undivided. Let no one deceive the brotherhood by a falsehood: let no one corrupt the truth of the faith by perfidious

---

[52] Henry Chadwick, *The Early Church* (London: Penguin Books, 1984), p. 118.

prevarication. The episcopate is one, each part of which is held by each one for the whole.[53]

Due to its very nature the Church cannot be divided; Christ underlined that unity by first bestowing the power of the keys on St. Peter so that "He arranged by His authority the origin of that unity, as beginning from one."[54] St. Cyprian then goes on to explain that the power of the keys was passed to the rest of the apostles, for "assuredly the rest of the apostles were also the same as was Peter, endowed with a like partnership both of honor and power; but the beginning proceeds from unity."[55]

For St. Cyprian all bishops shared in the Petrine powers, with the local Church and its bishop containing the totality of the universal Church. This vision of Church structure is reflected in St. Ignatius of Antioch, martyred circa 110 A.D.: "Where the bishop is to be seen, there let all his people be; just as wherever Jesus Christ is present, we have the catholic Church."[56] To this day the Orthodox Church still retains the essential catholicity of the early Church where the focus of unity is the bishop.

---

[53] *On the Unity of the Catholic Church*, 5, in *Ante-Nicene Fathers* (Peabody, MA: Hendrickson, 1994), vol. 5, p. 422.

[54] *On the Unity of the Catholic Church*, 4, p. 422.

[55] Ibid.

[56] *Early Christian Writings* (Harmondsworth, England:Penguin Books, 1987), p. 103.

THE CHURCH OF THE APOSTLES AND MARTYRS

As with St. Augustine's *Unity of the Church*, St. Cyprian in his work does not mention a single word about Rome, the necessity of communion with Rome, Rome as a center of unity, or Rome's supreme universal jurisdiction. Like St. Augustine, St. Cyprian is completely unconscious of Rome enjoying any special authority or jurisdiction over the universal Church. Had they been so conscious, then certainly these treatises on Church unity would have been the place to expound it.

A great deal of controversy has swirled around chapter 4 of St. Cyprian's *On the Unity of the Catholic Church*, due to the existence of two recensions. The longer recension is known as the *Primacy Text* because it stresses that "primacy was given to Peter" by Christ and that "those who abandon the chair of Peter cannot belong to the Church." Some scholars have suggested that since the longer text seems to favor papal primacy it must be an interpolation; however, others have suggested that St. Cyprian himself may have altered the text in order to avoid just such a misunderstanding, as the following illustrates:

> The mistake of earlier historians was that they identified the chair of Peter with the see of Rome. It appears that Cyprian was already aware of such a misunderstanding, and for this reason he removed those expressions and gave the text the short form.

CHAPTER II

What Cyprian wished to say was that in the famous verse of *Matthew* 16:18, "Upon this rock (*petra*) I will build my Church," the rock and chair of Peter is the faith, and since the faith is one, the see is also one. In this one see all the apostles take part, as well as their successors.... Therefore the important problems of the church can be solved only by a common decision of all the bishops in synod.[57]

In 253 Pope Cornelius died, and it was with his successor Stephen that St. Cyprian entered into the celebrated controversy over the rebaptism of heretics. It was a long-standing practice in the Church of North Africa and of Asia Minor to rebaptise all those who wished to enter the Church from heretical sects. For St. Cyprian, only the Church can validly baptize "...because in the holy Church is the one water which makes sheep."[58] Therefore, "...I answer, that no heretics and schismatics at all have any power or right."[59] Pope Stephen countered that baptism by water in the name of the Trinity was valid irrespective of who performed it, and those who were baptized outside the Church should be received by the laying on of hands.

In 256 a Council was convened in Carthage with seventy-one bishops in attendance reaffirming

---

[57] *The Encyclopedia of Religion* (New York: Macmillan Publishing Company, 1987), vol. 4, p. 188.
[58] *Epistle* 70:2.
[59] *Epistle* 75:1.

the necessity of rebaptism. St. Cyprian then sent a polite letter to Pope Stephen, written in a style of complete equality, informing him of the Council's decision while at the same time reminding him that each bishop has freedom of responsibility in the administration of his own Church. He also tells Stephen in so many words that perhaps on this issue, in the interest of peace, they should just agree to disagree:

> We have brought these things, dearest brother, to your knowledge, for the sake of our mutual honour and sincere affection; believing that, according to the truth of your religion and faith, those things which are no less religious than true will be approved by you. But we know that some will not lay aside what they have once imbibed, and do not easily change their purpose; but, keeping fast the bond of peace and concord among their colleagues, retain certain things peculiar to themselves, which have once been adopted among them. In which behalf we neither do violence to, nor impose a law upon, any one, since each prelate has in the administration of the Church the exercise of his will free, as he shall give an account of his conduct to the Lord. We bid you, dearest brother, ever heartily farewell.[60]

Pope Stephen's reply raised the temperature of the debate to white heat "with Stephen denouncing

---

[60] *Epistle* 71:3.

CHAPTER II

Cyprian as Antichrist."[61] Cyprian fumed at the "obstinacy" of "Stephen our brother," whose "error" is "haughtily assumed" and "contradictory." "But what is that blindness of soul, what is that degradation of faith, to refuse to recognize the unity which comes from God the Father, and from the tradition of Jesus Christ the Lord and our God!" "But it happens, by a love of presumption and of obstinacy, that one would rather maintain his own evil and false position, than agree in the right and true which belongs to another."[62] It was during this bitter controversy that Pope Stephen became the first Bishop of Rome to appeal to Matthew 16:18 "Thou art Peter..." in order to assert his see's supreme jurisdiction over the Church.

St. Cyprian responded to all this by holding an even larger Council at Carthage towards the end of 256, and in his opening speech to the eighty-seven assembled bishops he roundly denounced the claims of Pope Stephen:

> It remains, that upon this same matter each of us should bring forward what we think, judging no man, nor rejecting any one from the right of communion, if he should think differently from us. For neither does any of us set himself up as a bishop of bishops, nor by tyrannical terror does any compel his colleague to the necessity of obedience; since

---

[61] Chadwick, p. 120.
[62] *Epistle* 73:1,3,4,10.

every bishop, according to the allowance of his liberty and power, has his own proper right of judgment, and can no more be judged by another than he can judge another. But let us all wait for the judgment of our Lord Jesus Christ, who is the only one that has the power both of preferring us in the government of His Church, and of judging us in our conduct there.[63]

The claim of supreme jurisdiction by the Bishop of Rome was rejected by the Council's unanimous affirmation for the practice of rebaptism.

For Cyprian, the collegial structure of the Church, i.e., all bishops sharing power, is based on Divine Law, as he explains with a pointed reproof to those bishops who would set themselves over their peers:

....through the changes of times and successions, the ordering of bishops and the plan of the Church flow onwards; so that the Church is founded upon the bishops, and every act of the Church is controlled by these same rulers. Since this, then, is founded on the divine law, I marvel that some, with daring temerity, have chosen to write to me as if they wrote in the name of the Church.[64]

---

[63] *The Seventh Council of Carthage under Cyprian,* in *Ante-Nicene Fathers,* vol. 5, p. 565.

[64] *Epistle* 26:1.

CHAPTER II

This controversy faded away with the death of Stephen later in the year, and his successor St. Xystus wisely let the issue rest.

The Church ultimately settled the matter by rejecting the practice of rebaptism, but it was done in a forum that St. Cyprian would have recognized: by a General Council of the Church (the Council of Nicea, 325), not by one bishop. As St. Augustine himself insists, on the issue of rebaptism Cyprian would "undoubtedly have yielded if at any time the truth of the question had been placed beyond all dispute by the investigation and decree of a General Council."[65]

This celebrated controversy about the rebaptism of heretics "between Cyprian and Stephen certainly shows that they enjoyed equal moral authority in the eyes of their contemporaries."[66]

St. Cyprian corresponded with the well-respected St. Firmilian, bishop of the important see of Caesarea, regarding his controversy with Pope St. Stephen. St. Firmilian's reply is well worth reading:

---

[65] De Bapt. Contra donatistas, lib. (Migne) ii.P.L. 43:129
[66] *Encyclopedia of the Early Church* (New York: Oxford University Press, 1992), vol. 1, p. 212.

THE CHURCH OF THE APOSTLES AND MARTYRS

ST. FIRMILIAN, BISHOP OF CAESAREA (C 232-270)

But that they who are at Rome do not observe those things in all cases which are handed down from the beginning, and vainly pretend the authority of the apostles.[67]

The ancient city of Caesarea was the capital city of the Roman province of Cappadocia, now in modern-day Turkey. It is a haunting, surrealistic land of cone-shaped peaks and fretted ravines arrayed in striking colors of red, gold, green, and gray, where early Christian monastics had carved out chapels and monasteries. It is estimated that there are over 600 carved-out churches in Cappadocia. This rugged country of extreme climate and poor soil rendered it good for little else than rearing horses.

Because it lies almost in the center of a country with land connections to three continents and surrounded by the sea on three sides, it is easy to see why Caesarea was an important city and why Christianity came to it so early. St. Paul was imprisoned in Caesarea for a short time and Eusebius (c. 260-339), author of *The History of the*

---

[67] Epistle 74:6, St. Firmilian inter St. Cyprian.

Church, served as its bishop, as did St. Basil the Great after him.

Lying at the foot of Mt. Erciyes, the ancient city of Caesarea is now the booming farm and textile city of Kayseri, well known for its crafty carpet dealers. In winter months the city is filled with skiers who come to enjoy the excellent downhill runs on the nearby mountain. Unfortunately, very little of Caesarea itself remains.

St. Firmilian was one of the more influential bishops of his time; he was president of the first Council of Antioch, which was convened to examine the heresy of Paul, Bishop of Samasota. Cyprian consulted Firmilian during the Council of Carthage, which unanimously upheld the practice of rebaptism, when his controversy over this issue with Stephen, Bishop of Rome, was at its height.

Firmilian's reply was translated by Cyprian and is preserved in his *Epistle 74.* In its passionate condemnation of Pope Stephen it is more reminiscent of 16th century angry Protestant polemics. Firmilian's letter is certainly one of the more dramatic examples of the complete denial of 3rd century bishops of any supreme authority resting in the Bishop of Rome. He tells Cyprian, "You have replied most abundantly, that no one is so foolish as to believe that the apostles delivered this...But that they who are at Rome do not observe those things in all cases which are handed down from the beginning, and vainly pretend the authority of the apostles...What is the greatness of his error, and what the depth of his blindness, who says that remission of sins can be granted in the synagogues of heretics, and does not abide on the foundation of the one Church which was once based by Christ upon the rock..." (74:5,6,16). What follows is a complete denial of papal power based on Matthew 16:18, "Thou art Peter...." Firmilian, like most bishops, did not interpret this passage as conferring any special powers to the Bishop of Rome, as he very bluntly states:

> I am justly indignant at this so open and manifest folly of Stephen, that he who so boasts of the place of his episcopate, and contends that he holds the succession from Peter, on whom the foundations of the Church were laid, should introduce many other rocks and establish new buildings of many churches; maintaining that there is baptism in them by his authority. ...Nor does he understand that the truth of the Christian Rock is overshadowed, and in some measure abolished, by him when he thus betrays and deserts unity.[68]

Firmilian then goes on to excoriate Stephen in blistering language for breaking the peace of the Church.

---

[68] *Epistle* 74:17, St. Firmilian inter St. Cyprian.

CHAPTER II

Consider with what want of judgment you dare to blame those who strive for the truth against falsehood. ...For what strifes and dissensions have you stirred up throughout the churches of the whole world! Moreover, how great sin have you heaped up for yourself, when you cut yourself off from so many flocks! For it is yourself that you have cut off. Do not deceive yourself, since he is really the schismatic who has made himself an apostate from the communion of ecclesiastical unity. For while you think that all may be excommunicated by you, you have excommunicated yourself alone from all; and not even the precepts of an apostle have been able to mould you to the rule of truth and peace.[69]

All this is a world apart from the vision of the early Church, as espoused by Pope Leo XIII in his encyclical *Satis Cognitum,* where the supreme jurisdiction of Rome is "...the venerable and constant belief of every age" recognized "always and everywhere by all."

THE COLLEGIAL TRADITION

We can "declare with the confidence of a fearless voice that which under Government of our Lord God and Savior Jesus Christ has been ratified by a Council of the universal Church." St. Augustine, *De Bapt. Contra Donatistas*, lib, vii. P.L. 43:242, 243.

---

[69] *Epistle* 74:24, St. Firmilian inter St. Cyprian.

THE CHURCH OF THE APOSTLES AND
MARTYRS

"The west, while it accepted the decisions of the Ecumenical Councils, did not play a very active part in the Councils themselves,"[70] since all the Ecumenical Councils were held in the East, with an overwhelming presence of eastern bishops conducting their proceedings in Greek. As British historian Judith Herrin writes, "As few bishops of Rome had bilingual skills, they were increasingly dependent on Latin translations of Greek theological texts. Although canon law was recognized as fundamental to a universal faith, Rome had no complete Latin version of the first four oecumenical councils until the sixth century. Full participation in the process of defining dogma and establishing ecclesiastical discipline was therefore denied to the See of St. Peter, for without a complete knowledge of past rulings it was powerless."[71]

It is interesting to speculate that if, in the West, London and Paris had also been Patriarchal sees instead of only Rome, the West might have successfully preserved the collegial tradition. These additional sees might have acted as a brake on the development of a papal monarchy with its enormous centralized power and thus averted the Protestant Revolt. Instead, the rising floodwaters of

---

[70] Ware, p. 55.
[71] Judith Herrin, *The Formation of Christendom* (Princeton, New Jersey: Princeton University Press, 1989), pp. 104-105.

a spiritually disaffected European people lapped around the feet of powerful, overconfident Renaissance popes, too detached and removed to notice the danger.

Roman Catholics claim that a Supreme Pontiff, speaking with an authoritative voice, is necessary for the preservation of doctrine and tradition and it is only this that provides the Church with a rock of certitude. However, I would suggest that in the nine hundred years since Rome and the Orthodox Church have separated, it is the Orthodox Church in maintaining the conciliar form of government that has provided the greater witness to the liturgical and dogmatic traditions of the Early Church.

The Landscape is Different

In Orthodoxy, however, it is not merely the answers that are different--the questions themselves are not the same as in the west. Timothy Ware, *The Orthodox Church.*[72]

This is one side of the coin

AUGUSTINIANISM – THE GREAT DIVIDE

When Roman Catholics or Protestants look closely at the Orthodox Church, they realize very quickly that the religious landscape is different. For the concept of a faith based on a legal relationship with God that permeates their own churches is absent, thus giving the Orthodox Church an entirely different perspective. Instead of justification and the justice of God, the Orthodox Church's central theology is based on His love and the beauty and goodness of His creation. Therefore, as theologian Ernst Benz observes, "the major themes of the Orthodox faith are the apotheosis, sanctification, rebirth, re-creation and transfiguration of man; and not only man, but also

---

[72] Timothy Ware, *The Orthodox Church,* (Harmondsworth, England, Penguin Books, 1973), p. 9.

the whole universe—for the Eastern Church has a characteristically cosmic approach."[73]

As Professor Benz points out, the legalistic attitude that developed in the Western Church had its origins both in the ancient Roman relationship with their gods and in "the interpretation of redemption given by St. Paul in his Epistle to the Romans."[74] Paul was writing to Jewish Christians who were well versed in the Mosaic Law, which revealed God's righteousness, and was therefore addressing their concerns about God's justice and their duties towards Him.

St. Paul's doctrine of justification as found in *Romans* did not take root in the Eastern Church, which maintained a balance between the mysticism of St. Paul and the Gospel of St. John-- hence, "There is little emphasis upon justification."[75] It was St. Augustine who took Paul's doctrine of justification and created and defined a legal relationship between God and man. Henceforth, man's redemption and salvation would be defined in legal terms of responsibilities, duties, and punishments towards an exacting, just God. Given the Western churches' somewhat gloomy doctrine of Original Sin, it is understandable why

---

[73] Ernst Benz, *The Eastern Orthodox Church* (Garden City, New York: Anchor Books, 1963), p. 48.

[74] Ibid., p. 43.

[75] Ibid., p. 48.

people took such a morbid interest in their obligations. The famous Orthodox theologian St. John of Damascus (c.700-750) "does not even mention the idea of justification. So the Orthodox Church was never prompted to assert that the necessity for God's incarnation arose logically out of the doctrine of satisfaction:[76] the very groundwork for such a doctrine was lacking."[77]

In fact, it was a lawyer, Tertullian, who first defined the doctrine of Original Sin in the second century, and Augustine who elaborated it into a whole scheme of Redemption and Salvation. Here Augustine argued that the human race is under "a harsh necessity" of committing sin, and that "man's nature was overcome by the fault into which it fell, *and so came to lack freedom.*"[78] This pessimistic view flowed from the belief that the human race was not only wounded by Adam's fall, but also *inherited his guilt* and thus was deprived of God's grace. Therefore, as Augustine explained, unbaptized infants who die "shall not have life, but the wrath of God abideth on them. Whence could this result to those who clearly have no sins of their

---

[76] Satisfaction is the doctrine that the sufferings and death of Christ satisfied the requirements of God's justice. (Benz, p. 46.)
[77] Benz, p. 51.
[78] "On the Perfection of Man's Righteousness," iv (9), as quoted from Timothy Ware, *The Orthodox Church* (Harmondsworth, England: Penguin Books, 1973), p. 228.

own, if they are not held to be obnoxious to original sin?"[79]

Augustine taught that original sin is only transmitted through lust. While he admitted that the sexual act between husband and wife (providing it is only for procreation) is perfectly legitimate, "yet it cannot be effected without the ardor of lust." As Augustine explains:

> Wherefore the devil holds infants guilty who are born, not of the good by which marriage is good, but of the evil of concupiscence, which, indeed, marriage uses aright, but at which even marriage has occasion to feel shame. Marriage is itself "honorable in all" the goods which properly appertain to it; but even when it has its "bed undefiled" (not only by fornication and adultery, which are damnable disgraces, but also by any of those excesses of cohabitation such as do not arise from any prevailing desire of children, but from an overbearing lust of pleasure, which are venial sins in man and wife), yet, whenever it comes to the actual process of generation, the very embrace which is lawful and honorable cannot be effected without the ardor of lust...and that on this very account it produces shame. ...Now from this

[79] "A Treatise on the Merits and Forgiveness of Sins, and on the Baptism of Infants," Book 1, chap. 28, *The Nicene and Post-Nicene Fathers, Second Series,* Volume 5, *Augustin: Anti-Pelagian Writings* (Peabody, Mass.: Hendrickson, 1994), p. 25.

concupiscence whatever comes into being by natural birth is bound by original sin....[80]

The teaching of Augustine that unbaptized babies incur the wrath of God and damnation violated even Medieval Europe's sense of justice. Therefore, St. Thomas Aquinas introduced Limbo, (Limbus Infantum or Puerum) into Roman Catholic theology, as a place where infants are consigned who die without actual sin (personal sin)–but who did not have their original sin washed away by baptism. While Limbo is not hell, they are nevertheless for eternity "...excluded from the full blessedness of the beatific vision...."[81] This teaching was declared *de fide* by the Second Council of Lyons (1274) and confirmed by the Council of Florence (1439).

By contrast, the Orthodox Church has never held the view that unbaptized infants, "because tainted with original guilt, are consigned by the just God to the everlasting flames of Hell."[82] As a result, the Orthodox Church has never had the necessity for a place like Limbo. Augustine's views that sexual intimacy between husband and wife should only be for the procreation of children, thus denying any emotional, loving value, dominated

---

[80] Ibid., Chap. 27, pp. 274-275.

[81] John A. Hardon, S.J., *Pocket Catholic Dictionary* (Garden City, New York: Image Books, 1985), p. 228.

[82] Timothy Ware, *The Orthodox Church* (Harmondsworth, England: Penguin Books, 1973), p. 229.

the Western Church until the late nineteenth century.

Unfortunately for the early Western Church, Augustine was the only main theologian they had—whereas in the Eastern Church there were many; thus their theology, especially on salvation, was more balanced. As Father John Meyendorff comments, "There is no question, in patristic theology, of an inherited guilt transmitted to the human race through the sin of Adam. What is inherited by the entire human nature is slavery to death and corruption.... Instead of the Augustinian idea of the inherited guilt—only personal sins can produce guilt—the Fathers spoke of a *personal* power of death and corruption, that of the Devil, from which Christ came to liberate man, 'trampling down death by death.'"[83]

Thus the Orthodox Church's view of man's condition is more optimistic, for it teaches that the image of God in man is "distorted by sin, but never destroyed. In the words of a hymn sung by the Orthodox at the Funeral Service for the laity: 'I am the image of Thine inexpressible glory, even though I bear the wounds of sin.' And because he

---

[83] John Meyendorff, *Catholicity and the Church* (Crestwood, New York: St. Vladimir's Seminary Press, 1983), p. 72.

still retains the image of God, man still retains free will, although sin restricts his scope."[84]

It is this more optimistic view of the human condition that allows the Orthodox Church to venerate as saints those just men and women of the Old Testament, who without undergoing the grace of baptism were still capable of performing works pleasing to God.

Augustine's highly individualistic theology did not go unchallenged in the Western Church. St. Vincent of Lerins in his celebrated *Commonitorium* took strong exception against the dominant influence of Augustinian thought, which appeared to overwhelm and submerge the theological thought of contemporaries. Only that doctrine is binding, he wrote, which is held "everywhere, always and by all" (*quod semper, quod ubique, quod ab omnibus creditum*). He forcefully reminds those who pleaded that Augustine only "developed" dogma, that dogma can only mature-- not change into something else. It, therefore, "must truly be a development, and not a transformation of the faith. Understanding, knowledge, and wisdom must grow and develop in the same dogma, the same sense, the same meaning," and always adhering to the dictum of *universality, antiquity, and consent.*

---

[84] Ware, p. 229.

CHAPTER III

The Council of Orange (529) approved Augustine's doctrine of original sin in Canons 1-8, i.e., that freedom is "vitiated" in the children of Adam "and needs grace even to obtain the 'beginning of faith' (*initium fidei*), or the desire to be saved. By itself, fallen nature is not capable of any good work deserving salvation."[85] Historian John Meyendorff offers an Orthodox perspective:

> It remains, however, that--in spite of its moderation --the Council of Orange, whose decrees received the approval of pope Boniface II, confirmed the eminence of St. Augustine to the West, thereby disarming his critics. Later, the decrees will be used to bring about many theological impasses and tragic disputes. In retrospect, it would seem that the authority of St. Augustine himself would have been better served had it not been so absolute, so exclusive in the West, and had the second-rate theologians, who were his disciples in the fifth and sixth centuries, been more attentive to the truly catholic and cautious legacy of the monks of Lerins and their references to the faith of the Church held "by all, everywhere, at all times," a faith which could never be exhausted by a single local interpretation, however prestigious and respectable, like that of Augustinianism.[86]

The legalistic theology of the Western Church had wide implications, in that it so thoroughly

---

[85] John Meyendorff, *Imperial Unity and Christian Divisions* (Crestwood, New York: St. Vladimir's Seminary Press, 1989), p. 138.
[86] Ibid., p. 139.

permeated its doctrines--indulgences being one example. In expanding on this theme Professor Benz comments:

> The legalistic temper of Western Christianity has, characteristically, enlarged upon the idea of eternal damnation to a point quite alien to the Orthodox Church. Both Thomas Aquinas and Calvin in describing the bliss of the saved, suggest that one of the pleasures of heaven will consist in looking down upon the torments of the damned, for do not these torments glorify divine justice? Such attitudes, following as they do from the legalistic thinking of the West, are not to be found in the work of Eastern religious thinkers.[87]

The logical conclusion to be drawn from the above is that "the idea of justice has completely triumphed over the idea of love."

THE PRIMACY OF LOVE

Dearly beloved, let us love one another, for charity is of God. And every one that loveth is born of God and knoweth God. *I John 4:7*

If God were to treat us only with justice, then very few of us would merit eternal salvation. Therefore, the central theme that permeates

---

[87] Benz, p. 52.

Orthodox theology and thus saturates her liturgical prayers and hymns is the love and mercy of God. In the hierarchy of spiritual values, humility ranks first in the Orthodox Church as being the mother of all virtues. She, therefore, reminds her children of their sinful state, with numerous petitions and pleadings for God's mercy and for "a good defense before the dread judgment seat of Christ."

The primacy of love in the Orthodox Church probably finds one of its greatest expressions in St. John Chrysostom's catechetical sermon on the parable of the workers in the vineyard (Matt. 20:1-16) which is read in every church on the eve of Pascha. As Ernst Benz explains, "It is a triumphal hymn of the victory of love. Awareness of the overflowing fullness of divine love drives away all thought of any schemes of reckoning and satisfaction. Divine grace is bestowed as generously upon those who are called in the eleventh hour as upon those who were called in the eighth and ninth hours. 'Ye who are first and ye who are last, receive your reward. Rich and poor, rejoice together. Ye who are dutiful and ye who are neglectful, honor the day. Ye who have fasted and ye who have not fasted, today is the day of your rejoicing. The table is laden; let all partake! The calf is fattened; let none depart hungry. All may partake in the feast of faith. All may partake of the wealth of goodness. Let none complain of poverty, for the kingdom for all is come. Let none mourn transgressions, for forgiveness has risen radiant from the grave. Let none fear death, for the Savior's death has freed us from death.'"[88]

This view of salvation is far removed from the doctrine of justification and the legal relationship between God and man.

SCHOLASTICISM AND RATIONALISM

The Scholastics have concocted about God some problems so ridiculous you would think they were joking, and some statements so blasphemous you would think they were jeering. Thomas More, *The Praise of Folly*.[89]

In addition to Augustinian theology, a further cause of division with Eastern Christendom was the development of a method of inquiry called Scholasticism (from the word scholastic, i.e., schoolmen). By integrating the logic of the Greek philosopher Aristotle with theology, they created a new methodology with which they thought they could plumb the mysteries of the Christian faith. This great synthesis of rational philosophy and theology was based on the abstract syllogistic method of inquiry employed by Aristotle. This is a

---

[88] Benz, pp. 51-52.
[89] Richard Marius, *Thomas More* (New York, New York: Vintage Books, 1985), p. 149.

"form of reasoning in which a conclusion is drawn from two given or assumed propositions (premises): a common or middle term is present in the two premises but not in the conclusion, which may be invalid (e.g., *all trains are long; some buses are long; therefore some buses are trains:* the common term is *long).*"[90]

Armed with this new rational methodology, the medieval Scholastics believed they could illumine the depths of the Christian faith with logical proofs and discover the very boundaries between faith and reason. The greatest exponents of this new methodology were Peter Abelard (1079-1142) and the Dominican friars St. Albertus Magnus (1200-1280) and St. Thomas Aquinas (1225-1274).

Scholasticism represented a major break with the Platonic and Augustinian tradition of the Church Fathers, whose theology was primarily liturgical and contemplative. St. Bernard of Clairvaux (1090-1153) championed the traditional, mystical approach to theology with its primacy of the heart and took "an uncompromising stand against the rising tide of scholasticism among his contemporaries. He criticized Abelard, who had presumed to find reason for virtually every subject ('even of those things which are above reason,' to

---

[90] *The Concise Oxford Dictionary of Current English*, Ninth Edition (Oxford: Clarendon Press, 1995).

borrow Bernard's phrase)."[91] He was to find allies in the Franciscans who also distrusted "the long chains of syllogistic reasoning so confidently constructed by Aristotle's Dominican admirers."[92]

According to the philosopher and medievalist Etienne Gilson, Anselm and other scholastics "remain famous in the history of theology for their recklessness in giving rational demonstrations of all revealed truths.... This bold ambition to procure necessary reasons for the revealed dogmas had never entered the mind of Augustine."[93] However, "once the process had started, there was nothing to stop it, and by the end of the eleventh century the practice of scholastic debate was emerging as a central feature of the educational system."[94]

Theology was no longer only pursued in prayerful meditation and the liturgy, but was now an academic discipline of the universities. Doctrine was now "analyzed, defined, and codified in a way for which there is no parallel...But the most exciting feature, from the point of view of speculative thinkers, was the possibility that the

---

[91] Aristeides Papadakis in collaboration with John Meyendorff, *The Christian East and the Rise of the Papacy* (Crestwood, NY: St. Vladimir's Seminary Press, 1994), p. 62.

[92] William H. McNeill, *The Rise of the West* (Chicago, Illinois: The University of Chicago Press, 1963), p. 552.

[93] E. Gilson, *Reason and Revelation in the Middle Ages* (New York, 1938) as quoted by Papadakis, p. 27.

[94] R.W. Southern, *Medieval Humanism*, as quoted by Papadakis, p. 12.

CHAPTER III

relationship between the three Persons (of the Trinity) could be clarified by dialectical methods."[95]

By the fourteenth century the attempted synthesis of faith and reason was clearly unraveling. As others have noted, the "Middle Ages were called upon to witness the total wreck of both scholastic philosophy and scholastic theology as the necessary upshot of the final divorce of reason and revelation,"[96] "and the verbal extravagances of late scholastic philosophy–'How many angels can dance on the head of a pin?'--resembled the flamboyant over-decoration of late Gothic architecture in a more than metaphorical sense. In both cases, the structural lines and central purpose became obscured by a façade of excessive ornament and exhibitionist virtuosity."[97]

Desiderius Erasmus (1466-1536), Catholic humanist and one of the greatest figures of the Renaissance, leveled his biting wit at the more extreme forms of Scholasticism:

> They will explain the precise manner in which original sin is derived from our first parents; they will study you in what manner, by what degrees and in how long a time our Savior was conceived in the

---

[95] Colin Morris, *The Papal Monarchy (The Western Church from 1050 to 1250)* (Oxford: Clarendon Press, 1991), pp. 362, 365.
[96] Gilson, p. 87.
[97] McNeill, p. 552.

78

Virgin's womb, and demonstrate how in the consecrated wafer the accidents (appearance of the bread) can exist without the substance (the reality of the bread). Nay, these are accounted trivial, easy questions, they have greater difficulties behind, which, nevertheless, they solve with as much expedition as the former--namely, whether supernatural generation requires any instant of time?...Whether God, who took our nature upon him in the form of a man, could as well have become a woman, a devil, an ass, a gourd or a stone?[98]

Scholasticism, in turning theology into a classroom discipline, succeeded in draining it of its mysticism, thus giving the Christian faith in the West a dry, arid, brittle quality.

The Orthodox Church, however, has always maintained a mystical approach to theology, declaring that certain things are above human reason. "She veils and covers what the Latin Church lays open and exhibits. She feels reluctant to regulate the approach to the holy mysteries by precise disciplinary canons and to utter too detailed statements on the nature of such and such (e.g., on the Eucharistic Presence). This indefiniteness has a very simple explanation. The Orthodox Church wants a mystery to remain a

---

[98] "The Encomium Moriae, Desiderius Erasmus," as quoted in Jordan Bajis, *Common Ground* (Minneapolis, Minnesota: Light and Life Publishing Company, 1989), p. 25.

'mystery', and not to become a theorem, or a juridical institution."[99]

While we have been discussing one of two main forms of Scholasticism known as *theologism,* i.e., all aspects of the faith can be rationally explained, the other school of thought, which was a final development within the Scholastic tradition, was *nominalism.* This school taught that human reason was insufficient to explain revelation. Its chief proponent was William of Ockham (1300-1347), who held that "God eluded the theologians, and men deceived themselves if they thought otherwise."[100]   It was the Protestant Reformers who seized this line of reasoning and used it as the basis for their doctrines of *sola fide* (by faith alone) and *sola scriptura* (by scripture alone).[101]

In abandoning the tradition of the Fathers, "Western theologians now came to employ new categories of thought, a new theological method, and a new terminology which the East did not understand. To an ever-increasing extent the two

---

[99]By a Monk of the Eastern Church, *Orthodox Spirituality*, 2nd edition (Crestwood, New York: St. Vladimir's Seminary Press, 1996), p. 31.

[100] Friedrich Heer, *The Medieval World, Europe 1100-1350* (New York: Mentor Books, The New American Library, 1963), p. 276.

[101] Bajis, p. 37.

sides were losing a common 'universe of discourse.'" [102]

For new Orthodox Christians, especially if they are coming from a Protestant or Roman Catholic background, it is vital to understand these differences and to reach beyond the Protestant revolt of the sixteenth century and the Roman Catholic Counter-Reformation that define the boundaries of our religious experience; to move beyond the medieval Scholastics to the Patristic Fathers and their mystical, contemplative approach to theology: "If you are a theologian, you will pray truly. And if you pray truly, you are a theologian."[103] If we are to develop a true Orthodox mentality, then we must shed our Scholastic-based "categories of thought and methodology" and turn to the writings of the Fathers. It is only from the feet of men such as these that the spiritual richness of the Orthodox faith will come alive.

Another great change occurred in the West during the Middle Ages and severed a shared tradition with the East -- that of religious toleration. On this subject we turn to Friedrich Heer, Professor of History, University of Vienna:

---

[102] Ware, pp. 71-72.
[103] See p. 40.

CHAPTER III

The fact that toleration can be discussed at all in connection with the Middle Ages is striking enough; it underlines the magnitude of the metamorphosis which transformed the "open" Middle Ages of the expansive twelfth century into the increasingly narrow and constricted later Middle Ages.

Toleration implied toleration of pagans and heretics, of men of different faiths living within or on the fringes of a Christian society. As with many other matters, the traditional teaching about toleration inherited from the Early Church was conflicting and ambiguous in the extreme. Great minds such as Origen and the majority of the Greek Fathers had completely rejected the idea of using force against pagans and "heretics," in which they were supported in the West by Tertullian, Lactantius and Salvian. They also favored toleration in the case of individuals, as did Hilary, Ambrose, Augustine, and in fact all the great authorities of early Christian theology. It became an acknowledged maxim that no violence might be perpetrated on a man's conscience: "a man could believe only of his own free will".... Thomas Aquinas urged the severest punishment for heretics, and also for *relapsi,* back-sliders, on the grounds that heresy was an evil so infectious that its practitioners must be eradicated as thoroughly as possible. Referring to the sack of Constantinople he comments that one interesting consequence of the victory of the Western Church over the Eastern (in any case an illusory victory) was the way the more magnanimous Greek Fathers were now reinterpreted in the West. Thomas

THE LANDSCAPE IS DIFFERENT

Aquinas alleged that St. John Chrysostom had demanded that Arius be condemned to death, and that this was the origin of the death penalty for heretics![104]

Professor Heer's exclamation mark refers to the fact that the arch-heretic Arius died c. 335 while St. John Chrysostom lived 347-407.

THE LOSS OF CHRISTIAN HELLENISM

If the Church had chosen the Greek way she would have found Christ's way far easier and she might with Him have disdained temporal power. But she chose the Roman way. Edith Hamilton, *The Echo of Greece*.[105]

The Orthodox Church is the only church left that can present to a neo-pagan world the fullness of Christ's Gospel. "It is this fullness and depth of Christ's revelation that our age desperately needs and which the Christian Hellenism of Orthodoxy alone can give. The loss of the Hellenic heritage by the Western Church as a result of the barbaric

---

[104] Heer, pages 146-147.
[105] Edith Hamilton, *The Echo of Greece* (New York: W.W. Norton & Company, 1964), p. 215.

invasions has been costly to western civilization."[106]

Greece was the birthplace of the modern spirit. "They were the first Westerners; the spirit of the West, the modern spirit, is a Greek discovery and the place of the Greeks is in the modern world,"[107] at the center of which was an uncompromising, relentless belief in the dignity and value of individual man. The early Church readily fused these insights with the Gospel message, to which the Orthodox Church has been an enduring witness. Had the Western Church clung to this "Christian Hellenism," Western Christianity may have avoided some of its uglier chapters, as the American historian Edith Hamilton writes:

> If the Church had chosen the Greek way she would have found Christ's way far easier and she might with Him have disdained temporal power. But she chose the Roman way....To the Romans the first essentials were obedience to authority and disciplined control.... The Roman way led the Church to supreme power, power over heaven and hell as well as earth.... If the Church had chosen the Greek way some of the most terrible pages in history might never have had to be written. The

---

[106] Rev. Eusebius A. Stephanou, *An Orthodox Interpretation of the Crisis of Western Society* (Brookline, Massachusetts: Holy Cross Seminary Press), p. 14.
[107] Edith Hamilton, *The Greek Way* (New York, NY: The Modern Library, 1961), p. 19.

Inquisition, the prisons people were flung into, the ways the condemned were killed, the massacres of nonconformists—all this was fostered and favored by the conviction that human beings generally were bad and ought to suffer. The conception of God, which developed through these ruthless centuries, was calculated to do away with mercy and compassion in the hearts of His worshippers. It is phrased clearly in the Westminster Shorter Catechism, a subject for reverential study in Presbyterian households for hundreds of years. In it this statement is made: In Adam's fall 'mankind lost communion with God, are under His wrath and curses, and so made liable to all the miseries of this life, to death itself, and to the pains of hell for ever.' If God felt that way, it was clearly right for men to make objectionable people suffer. Whatever they did would be less than the pains of hell forever; men need not be more merciful and pitiful than God. If the Church had taken the Greek way that weight of human agony might never have been. A cruel God would not have been possible to Greeks.[108]

Edith Hamilton points out that formalism was another danger that could have been avoided, e.g., an excessive adherence to prescribed external forms such as confessions, creeds, or theologies. This rigid formalism that held words to be a more important expression of truth than the way people lived created a moral blindness in the Western Church. "The Inquisition put people to death not for

---

[108] Edith Hamilton, *The Echo of Greece* (New York, NY: W.W. Norton & Company, 1964), pp. 215-220.

living wickedly, but for making what to the Inquisitors were incorrect statements."[109]

Dr. John Thatcher of the Dumbarton Oaks Center of Byzantine Studies states: "There is in Orthodoxy an enormous potential, which when it bursts into its full glory again, will be one of the most magnificent forces for good existing in the world.... The Ecumenical Orthodox Church is a living organism and it has a great potential for good that the world needs."[110]

---

[109] Ibid., p. 221.
[110] As quoted in Stephanou, p. 20.

The Divine Liturgy

Thou, O Lord, hast chosen this house, for thy name to be called upon therein, that it might be a house of prayer and supplication for thy people. 1 Maccabees 7:37

Religious experience differs widely among people. For some, belief in God comes slowly over a long period, sometimes a lifetime; for others it is an instant "Damascus road" experience. For me, however, as a young boy growing up in Surrey, England, there never was a time that I did not feel the presence of God. This was not a feeling that ebbed and flowed, but an indefinable presence that was always there. As a choirboy at our local Anglican Church, with its carved wooden choirstalls, soaring stained glass windows, and flickering candles, I was able to express through the liturgical prayers and the hymns what I inwardly felt.

Thus, like most Christians, I had a liturgical approach to my faith that has now found its fulfillment in the magnificent liturgy of the Orthodox Church. For the Divine Liturgy or Eucharist is the inner life and soul of the Church. Her lifeblood flows from the true presence of Christ in the

CHAPTER IV

Eucharist that is celebrated at every Liturgy. Without His divine sacramental presence, the Church could not achieve her earthly mission. It is in the celebration of the Eucharist that we have the loving presence of God Who fills heaven and earth with His majestic glory.

The Orthodox Church teaches that His children are naturally liturgical because they are only fulfilled and perfected through loving and glorifying God in worship. Thus, for the Orthodox Church, the Divine Liturgy, the Eucharistic celebration of Christ's death and resurrection, is the hymn of the universe. It is the very heart of her faith. It is an earthly reflection of the eternal liturgy celebrated by the choirs of angels in Heaven before the throne of God.

The central point of the Divine Liturgy is the celebration of the Eucharist where the invisible reality of Christ's triumphant entry is lauded, surrounded by the Heavenly Hosts, "Attend, O Lord Jesus Christ our God, out of Thy holy dwelling-place, from the throne of glory of Thy Kingdom; and come to sanctify us, O Thou who sittest on high with the Father, and art here invisibly present with us...."

In his book *The Orthodox Church,* Sergius Bulgakov observes that "each of the historic branches of universal Christianity has received a special gift, a characteristic of its own. Catholicism has received the gift of organization and administration, Protestantism the ethical gift of probity of life and of intellectual honesty; while on the Orthodox peoples—and especially Byzantium and Russia—has fallen the gift of perceiving the beauty of the spiritual world."[111]

Many people attending an Orthodox Liturgy for the first time are struck by the length of the service and an overpowering sense of mystical sacredness. Where most Western liturgies tend to be somber and penitential, the Orthodox Church has retained the early Christian sense of rejoicing in Christ's victory over death and sin. Another distinguishing feature is that the Liturgy is chanted or sung, without any instrumental accompaniment, as it was in the early Church. In fact, the Church Fathers "offered strenuous opposition" to the use of musical instruments in liturgical settings.[112] Their introduction in Western churches was a revolutionary break with tradition.

IT ALL HANGS TOGETHER

Take but degree away, untune that string, And, hark! What discord follows! William Shakespeare, *Troilus and Cressida*, iii.109.

---

[111] Sergius Bulgakov, *The Orthodox Church* (Maitland , Florida: The Three Hierarchs Seminary Press , 1935), p. 149.
[112] *Encyclopaedia Britannica*, 1972, vol. 15, p. 1065.

CHAPTER IV

The Russian Primary Chronicle relates how the pagan prince Vladimir of Kiev in searching for the true religion sent emissaries to various countries of the world. After visiting the Muslim Bulgars and Rome, they arrived in Constantinople and observed the Divine Liturgy in the great church of Hagia Sophia (Holy Wisdom). "We knew not whether we were in heaven or on earth, for surely there is no such splendor or beauty on earth. We cannot describe it to you; only this we know that God dwells there among humans, and that their service surpasses the worship of all other places. For we cannot forġet that beauty."[113]

Here the Russian emissaries encountered that unique Orthodox ability to reflect the mystical splendor of the spiritual world in her Divine Liturgy: *We knew not whether we were in heaven or on earth.... For we cannot forget that beauty.* In succumbing to the beauty and majesty of the Divine Liturgy, the Russians displayed a characteristic Orthodox response, as Timothy Ware explains: "When they wanted to discover the true faith, the Russians did not ask about moral rules nor demand a reasoned statement of doctrine, but watched the different nations at prayer. The Orthodox approach to religion is fundamentally a liturgical approach, which

---

[113] As quoted in Timothy Ware, *The Orthodox Church,* p. 269.

understands doctrine in the context of divine worship."[114]

Orthodox dogma and theology, unlike the Protestant and Roman Catholic churches, are woven into the very fabric of her Liturgy. Doctrine and theology are not primarily relegated to classrooms for study and analysis, but form the lifeblood of her worship. It is this insistence that the Liturgy is the natural arena for doctrine and theology that gives the Orthodox Church her tremendous liturgical character and doctrinal cohesion. This distinctive quality was particularly noted by author Peter Hammond:

> Orthodox Christendom has never undergone an upheaval comparable to that which shattered the unity of the western world in the sixteenth century, not on account of the glacier of Turkish dominion which descended upon it a hundred years earlier, but because it had never known that separation of theology and mysticism, liturgy and personal devotion, which–when all is said as to the influence of political and economic factors–is required to explain the all-engulfing cataclysm of the Reformation.[115]

In this approach she reflects the ancient law of the Church, i.e., *lex orandi, lex credendi* - the law

---

[114] Ware, p. 271.
[115] Peter Hammond, *The Waters Of Marah* (London and Southampton, Great Britain: The Camelot Press, 1956), pp. 16-17.

CHAPTER IV

of prayer is the law of belief. Or as the monk Evagrius Ponticus (346-399) states: "If you are a theologian, you will pray truly. And if you pray truly, you are a theologian."[116]

It is precisely because doctrine and theology are woven into the very fabric of her worship that the Orthodox Church "often attributes to minute points of ritual an importance which astonishes Western Christians...if worship is the faith in action, then liturgical changes cannot lightly be regarded."[117] That liturgy guards and protects doctrine is a truth readily recognized by the 17th century Roman Catholic bishop historian Jacques Bossuet, for in his book *Histoire des Variations des Eglises Protestants* he describes how liturgical experimentation denied Protestants doctrinal cohesion, shattering them into numberless different denominations.

Thus it is that Orthodox Christians should continue to be zealous guardians of their Liturgy, for it is their priceless treasure, the very heart of their faith that they must pass on to their children intact. It would be hard to find a greater, more eloquent tribute to our Liturgy than that given by Roman Catholic Cardinal Ratzinger when he writes

---

[116] Evagrius, *On Prayer* 61.
[117] Daniel B. Clendenin, (ed.), *Eastern Orthodox Theology: A Contemporary Reader* (Grand Rapids, Michigan: Baker Books, 1995), p. 13.

that the Orthodox Church "does not see liturgy as developing or growing in history, but only the reflection of the eternal liturgy, whose light, through the sacred celebration, illumines our changing times with its unchanging beauty and grandeur."[118]

IN OUR FATHER'S HOUSE

I have loved, O Lord, the beauty of thy house; and the place where thy glory dwelleth. Psalm 25:8

When Orthodox Christians enter the Church, they make the sign of the cross and bow three times, saying:

Thou hast created me, O God, have mercy on me,

I have sinned without measure, have mercy on me,

God, be merciful to me a sinner.

Then "they venerate with a kiss: first, the icon of Christ, next, that of the Theotokos, and then ordinarily the icon of the feast-day or of the liturgical cycle, placed in evidence in the middle of the church." [119] In the early Church, the iconostasis was a low barrier adorned with icons that served

---

[118] *The Latin Mass,* Vol. 2, No. 1, Jan/Feb. 1993 (Fort Collins, Colorado: Foundation for Catholic Reform), p. 21.

[119] Michel Quenot, *The Icon: Window on the Kingdom* (Crestwood, New York: St. Vladimir's Seminary Press, 1991), p. 46.

as a partition, separating the sanctuary from the nave.

By the 15th century, with the addition of more and larger icons arranged in tiers, the iconostasis achieved the wall-like form as we now know it. The arrangement of the icons on the iconostasis are in a specified order rather than a haphazard creation. The icon of Christ is always to the right of the royal door (the large center door) and on the left side of the door is the Theotokos. St. John the Baptist occupies the space immediately to the right of Christ, while the patron saint of the church is found immediately to the left of the Theotokos. The archangels St. Gabriel and St. Michael, representing the heavenly host, are to be found on the deacon doors at either end of the iconostasis. These are the principal icons and as such are usually life-size.

THE ICON

Icons get under the skin of reality and convince us that they are showing the supernatural from the inside, precisely because they are so indifferent to the look, scale and color of reality. Marina Warner.[120]

---

[120] Anne Glyn-Jones, *Holding Up A Mirror* (London: Century Books, 1996), p. 10.

The icon has an important central role in the Liturgy of the Orthodox Church, for besides being frequently incensed they are on special occasions carried in procession. Furthermore, "everything that is taught by the Divine Liturgy, the hymns of the Church and the words of the reader, truly find a luminous commentary in the silence of the frescoes and icons."[121]

To perceive and comprehend Orthodox dogma, one must understand the central role the icon commands in the religious life of the Orthodox Church. Due to ignorance and misunderstanding, many people believe the veneration of icons to be idolatrous. However, the Second Council of Nicea (787) laid to rest any question of idolatry when it decreed that "the honour which is paid to the image passes on to that which the image represents, and he who reveres the image reveres in it the subject represented."[122]

Most people, when they encounter an icon for the first time, are struck by its strange, somewhat exotic "otherworldliness." Attempted comparisons with "realistic," Western religious art are impossible, due to the substantially different underlying aims of the two artistic traditions. The icon's primary role in Orthodox religious life is to

---

[121] Ibid., p. 47.

[122] *The Seven Ecumenical Councils* in *The Nicene and Post-Nicene Fathers,* Second Series, vol. 14, p. 550.

display "theology in imagery" through the colors used and symbolic language. The absence of naturalism in the icon is to unveil the spiritual reality of a universe transfigured by the Incarnation of Christ. This spiritual reality of a world transfigured is reflected symbolically in the portrayal of saints, as described by Michel Quenot in his book *The Icon*:

> Touched and sanctified by Divine grace, every organ of our senses has ceased to be the usual sensory organ of a biological man. The eyes are both animated and large, witnessing to the scripture verse of Ps 25:15, "My eyes gaze continually at the Lord,"...."because my eyes have seen Thy salvation" (Lk 2:30). They have been opened to marvel at the sublime and at the vision of the works of our Creator.

> Looking at the rest of the face we see the forehead, the nose, the ears, the mouth and also the cheeks, which are given deep wrinkles for ascetics, monks and bishops. The forehead is often rather convex and quite high, expressing both the power of the Spirit and of wisdom, which are inseparable from love. The nose is thin and elongated, giving a nobility to the face. It no longer detects the scents of this world, but only the sweet odor of Christ and the life-giving breath of the Spirit gushing from a throat and neck, which are disproportionately large. The mouth, being an extremely sensual organ, is always drawn finely and geometrically, eliminating its sensuality. The lips remain closed, because true

contemplation demands silence. As a sign of spirituality, according to Cyril of Jerusalem (d. 387), the small mouth stresses that "the body no longer needs earthly nourishment because it has become a spiritual wonder" (Migne, P.G. 33,613, *Catechesis* 18).

The ears, created to hear the commandments of the Lord, have become interiorized, and they no longer hear or listen to the sounds of this world. [123]

The icon finds its *raison d'être* in the knowledge that man is created "in the image of God," and thus bears the icon of God within himself. "This belief is so central to Orthodox theology and anthropology, the consciousness that man was imprinted with the image of God from the day of creation so dominant, that the idea of original sin never could become established within the Orthodox Church in its blunt Western form. Sin manifests itself as a distortion, a damaging, infecting and tainting of the image of God; but it cannot rob man of his original nobility. This is always his because he remains the image of God."[124]

In most Orthodox churches, especially in Europe, people stand throughout the Liturgy as they did in the early Church. In the West, "sitting as a posture for the faithful, was hardly thought of

[123] Michel Quenot, *The Icon, Window on the Kingdom* (Crestwood, New York: St. Vladimir's Seminary Press, 1991), p. 97.
[124] Benz, pp. 18-19.

CHAPTER IV

seriously in the churches of the Middle Ages, since
there was no provision made for seats.... it was not
till near the end of the Middle Ages that any
localities began to consider the possibility of the
people's sitting down."[125]

Standing adds an informal atmosphere without
detracting from the reverence and sacred
character, e.g., people can move about lighting
candles and changing position without unsettling
their fellow worshippers. Since becoming
Orthodox, whenever I visit Roman Catholic or
Protestant churches, it never fails to strike me how
pews introduce a stifling rigidity into the spirit of
worship. With military precision they march down
the nave of the church, enclosing and confining
each occupant in their limited space for the
duration of the service. It is an absolute travesty to
see them in some Orthodox churches, as it
severely limits or even eliminates many of the
liturgical gestures so inherent in Orthodox worship,
e.g., full prostrations. If these churches wish to
foster true Orthodox worship, then the pews should
be removed.

During a recent trip to Russia, we attended a
number of Orthodox churches where a strict dress
code applies – bare shoulders and shorts are

---

[125] Joseph A. Jungmann, S.J., *The Mass of the Roman Rite: Its Origins
and Development* (Westminster, Maryland: Christian Classics,
Inc, 1986), vol. 1, p. 241.

prohibited. It is interesting that in the poorer countries in which we have traveled, people still have a conscious regard that, when entering the House of God, one dresses modestly and well out of respect, something that many of their counterparts in the affluent West have lost. It is the tradition of the Church that only the very best is fitting for the worship of God: this is reflected in the extensive adornment one sees in most Orthodox churches, from the icons to the silver, gold, and silk vestments of the priest and the gold altar furnishings.

This rich, aesthetic setting that encompasses a refined formal Liturgy in the presence of the King of Kings is in jarring contrast to some members of the congregation who are more appropriately attired for the beach or a hike in the woods. One wonders if they would observe a different dress code were they to visit the Queen at Buckingham Palace or the President in the White House.

CHAPTER V

Frequently Asked Questions from Roman Catholics

WHY DOES THE ORTHODOX CHURCH PERMIT DIVORCE? IT SEEMS LIKE SUCH A MAJOR DEPARTURE FROM CHRISTIAN TRADITION.

Coming from Roman Catholicism, the Orthodox Church's position on divorce was a huge stumbling block for my wife and me, as it is for many Roman Catholics. The length of the following answer is a reflection of this, for it was only resolved after much study and contemplation. The teaching of the Orthodox Church on marriage and divorce is as follows:

The Holy Orthodox Church does, however, permit divorce and remarriage, quoting as her authority the words of the Savior: **For your hardness of heart Moses allowed you to divorce your wives, but from the beginning it was not so. And I say to you: Whoever divorces his wife except for unchastity, and marries another, commits adultery** (Matt. 19:8-9). Here Our Lord allows an

101

CHAPTER V

exception to the indissolubility of marriage, and so, too, the Church is willing to allow an exception.

While in principle the church regards the marriage bond as lifelong and indissoluble, and condemns the breakdown of marriage as a sin and as evil, she still desires to help the sinners and to allow them a second chance. Thus, when a marriage has ceased to be a reality, the Church does not insist on the preservation of a legal fiction. Divorce, therefore, is seen as an exceptional, but necessary concession to human weakness. Yet, while helping men and women to rise again after a fall, the Church does not view a second or a third marriage as being the same as the first and thus, in the ceremony for a second or third marriage, several joyful ceremonies are omitted and replaced by penitential prayers. Orthodox Canon Law permits a second or third marriage, but more than that is strictly forbidden.[126]

In the light of the Orthodox position, an understanding of the Roman Catholic teaching and its development is necessary in order to arrive at a clear picture. The general view of the Roman Catholic Church's position on the indissolubility of marriage is that of a "monolithic and unchanging doctrine." However, as American historian Norman Verberie (752)[127] and the Council of Compiegne

---

[126] *These Truths We Hold* (South Canaan, Pennsylvania: St. Tikhon's Seminary Press, 1986), p. 315.
[127] Roderick Phillips, *Putting Asunder–A History of Divorce in Western Society* (London: Cambridge University Press, 1988), p. 21.

FREQUENTLY ASKED QUESTIONS FROM ROMAN CATHOLICS

(757)[128] permitted divorce and remarriage, as did Theodore, Archbishop of Canterbury (668-690), and Pope Eugenius at the Roman synod in 826 for cases of adultery. "The important Penitential of Theodore (seventh century)" also made "allowances for remarriage, so that 'if a woman leaves her husband, despising him, and is unwilling to return and be reconciled to her husband, after five years, with the bishop's consent, he shall be permitted to take another wife'."[129] However, it was not until the twelfth century and beyond that the Church developed a consensus on the indissolubility of marriage. Only at the Council of Trent in 1563 did it enter canon law.[130] The Orthodox Church permitted divorce for reasons of adultery at the Council of Trullo (692).

Up to the eleventh century and even beyond, the canon law of the church "did not require any marriage formalities." For most people in Western Europe, marriage did not involve a church ceremony, but merely the blessing of the church:

> It thus became customary that parties planning to be married, before entering upon their life in common, would meet at the door of the church, but outside of

---

[128] Frances and Joseph Gies, *The Marriage and the Family in the Middle Ages* (New York, NY: Harper & Row, 1987), p. 57.
[129] Ibid., p. 22.
[130] Ibid., p. 24.

it (*in facie ecclesiae*), with the parish priest, who would then and there bestow upon them his blessing. The conclusion of marriage remained, however, the private transaction of the parties, consisting in their intentions from there on to be husband and wife (*sponsalia per verba de praesenti*). When followed by carnal consummation, this exchange of expressions of *consensus maritalis* would mature into the sacrament and the marriage would thus become indissoluble.[131]

The medieval practice of a church blessing is recorded in Geoffrey Chaucer's *Canterbury Tales,* where the Wife of Bath claims that "housbondes at chirche-dore I have had fyve."[132]

Drawing on the Book of Leviticus, the Western church laid down rules of consanguinity, i.e., rules that impeded marriage to those related by blood. However, advancing from the sixth century to the twelfth, the church expanded the degrees of consanguinity far beyond the Biblical injunctions to the seventh degree, e.g., men and women were forbidden marriage from the first to the sixth cousin (the Orthodox Church never accepted the seventh degree regulation).[133]

---

[131] *Encyclopaedia Britannica,* 1972, vol. 14, p. 927.
[132] Geoffrey Chaucer, *Canterbury Tales: The Prologue to the Wife of Bath's Tale,* ed. Vincent Hopper (Woodbury, New York: Barron's Educational Series, Inc., 1970), p. 384.
[133] Gies, p. 87.

FREQUENTLY ASKED QUESTIONS FROM
ROMAN CATHOLICS

This rule had daunting consequences on those of marriageable age, for "if in each generation each couple had married off one boy and one girl, which was lower than the real average in the eleventh and twelfth centuries, then a marriageable youth would be forbidden to marry 2,731 cousins of his own generation, even without counting their ancestors or descendants of marriageable age. In other words, whether he were a great lord marrying into his own class, or a peasant bound to the soil, he would be unable to marry all the marriageable girls he could possibly know and a great many more besides." [134]

When we consider the Middle Ages as basically a rural society of small static settlements of hamlets and villages, where people seldom ventured more than fifty miles from their birthplace, we can well sympathize with their predicament. Thus the potential for annulments, i.e., dissolving what would appear to be an indissoluble union through the discovery of cousinhood, must have been enormous.

The discovery of such an impediment in an unhappy marriage would be looked upon as fortuitous. A prime example of this would be the annulment of Eleanor of Aquitaine's fifteen-year marriage (producing several daughters) to Louis VII

---

[134] Phillips, pp. 5-6.

(1137-1180). It was while she accompanied him on the Second Crusade (1147-1149) that the estrangement between them began to take its toll. Louis accused Eleanor of infidelity with one of his generals. She accused Louis of being "more monk than king." Despite the efforts of the papacy to save the marriage, an annulment was granted after it was discovered that they were cousins of the fourth and fifth degree. Upon receiving the annulment, Eleanor immediately married Henry II of England.

In 1215 Pope Innocent III convened the Fourth Lateran Council which regularized marriages, e.g., insisting on mutual consent, church ceremony, declaration and publication of banns, and reducing the degrees of consanguinity from the seventh to the fourth. However, even by 1500, "there were still many peasants who were married by the simple rite of cohabitation."[135]

As mentioned earlier, indissolubility entered canon law at the Council of Trent in 1563. For the next four hundred years until the Second Vatican Council (1963-1965), the absolute indissolubility of marriage was rigorously applied. Seeking an annulment (a declaration from the church that due to some impediment a marriage never took place) became a lengthy and costly procedure that only celebrities or the very wealthy could pursue.

---

[135] Phillips, pp. 30-34. Also see Cantor, p. 419.

FREQUENTLY ASKED QUESTIONS FROM ROMAN CATHOLICS

Following the Second Vatican Council, the reasons for nullifying a marriage were expanded to unimaginable dimensions by the publication in 1964 of an influential doctoral dissertation by Father John Keating, currently bishop of Arlington, Virginia.

In his doctoral dissertation, Keating argued that psychological factors could provide grounds for an annulment, since one or both parties may have been "incapable of knowing what they were doing or incapable of assuming the fundamental responsibilities of marriage."[136] This could be due to such psychological reasons as "antisocial or narcissistic behavior," or "whether a person deliberated in a sufficient manner before consenting to marriage."[137] A well-circulated Catholic reference book reveals that in annulling marriages, tribunals consider such "deficiencies (as) gross immaturity and those affecting in a serious way the capacity to love, to have a true interpersonal conjugal relationship, to fulfill marital obligations, to accept the faith aspect of marriage." "While this interpretation of the law may strike some Catholics as reasonable and compassionate, it logically undermines the notion of consent, since an act of the will for which one may be held accountable is always open to question. Or in the

---

[136] *U. S. Catholic*, April 1997.
[137] Ibid.

words of a canon lawyer, 'There isn't a marriage in America we can't annul.'"[138]

Today nearly fifty percent of U.S. Catholic marriages end in divorce (about the same as the general population), with only ten percent of those seeking church annulments. In spite of this, the number of annulments has skyrocketed from only 338 in 1968 to 54,463 in 1994 with 90 percent being granted.[139] To many Catholics, an annulment is nothing more than a substitute for divorce, or as one prominent Catholic describes it, "it's an end run around Catholic teaching on the indissolubility of marriage."[140]

The Roman Catholic Church's controversial annulment process gained national attention, when Sheila Rauch Kennedy (an Episcopalian and former wife of Congressman Joseph P. Kennedy II) wrote a book, *Shattered Faith,* in which she criticized "the annulments procedure in ruling that a once happy marriage never existed in the eyes of God."[141] She further comments that "[I]t's not just saying that the marriage is over, which is what a divorce says, it's saying that what they gave their

---

[138] *Credo*, August 1997
[139] William F. Buckley, Jr., *Nearer My God* (New York, NY: Harcourt Brace & Company, 1998), p. 108.
[140] Ibid.
[141] *Time*, May 12, 1997, p. 36.

lives to—which was a sacramental union—never existed."[142]

That the annulment process didn't bathe Congressman Joseph P. Kennedy's character in a favorable light is attested by a *New Republic* commentator who observed that he "didn't possess the elementary judgment to be trusted with the most basic decision of his life. To most people around here, that means the Church thinks Joe Kennedy is too dumb for his marital vows to count. This isn't good."[143]

In the light of history, the Orthodox Church's position on divorce and remarriage is far more equitable, e.g., whether you are a prince or a pauper your treatment is the same, something that Sheila Rauch Kennedy readily recognizes when she comments, "We all know that marriages fail, but that doesn't mean they weren't marriages...I've talked to enough Catholics who seem to feel that some change is in order. As you may be aware, the Eastern Church, for second-time marriages, recognizes the distinction between the valid and sacramental. If you're going for a second marriage you can have a valid marriage but not a sacramental marriage. Which is what the Catholic Church does if a Catholic member marries

---

[142] *Credo*, August 1997.
[143] As quoted in *Credo*, August 1997.

someone who isn't baptized. It regards those marriages as valid but not sacramental. To me, separating the sacramental and valid would be a much better response to the very real dilemma that the Church has here in this country."[144]

WHAT IS THE POSITION OF THE ORTHODOX CHURCH ON THE DOCTRINE OF THE IMMACULATE CONCEPTION?

The Roman Catholic doctrine of the Immaculate Conception of Mary states that:

> ...the Blessed Virgin Mary, at the first instant of her conception, by a singular privilege and grace of the omnipotent God, in consideration of the merits of Jesus Christ, the Savior of mankind, was preserved free from all stain of original sin, has been revealed by God, and therefore is to be firmly and constantly believed by all the faithful. Pius IX, *Ineffabilis Deus,* December 8, 1854.

While the Orthodox Church has never delivered any formal teaching on this matter, they generally reject it because it is based on the false Augustinian belief that Adam's guilt is passed on to us through the conjugal act (see Chapter III, The Landscape is Different). Some Orthodox theologians have commented that such a belief

---

[144] Ibid.

demands an Immaculate Conception. Also the doctrine "seems to separate Mary from the rest of the descendants of Adam, putting her in a completely different class from all the other righteous men and women of the Old Testament."[145]

The Orthodox Church teaches that Mary's response was completely voluntary, i.e., the possibility had to exist for her saying *no,* thus making her not merely a "passive, but an active participant in the mystery." It is only after agreeing to the wishes of God at the Annunciation that she is then cleansed of all sin, thus becoming in the words of England's great poet William Wordsworth "our tainted nature's solitary boast."[146] For "if Christ is the New Adam, Mary is the New Eve, whose obedient submission to the will of God counterbalanced Eve's disobedience in Paradise. 'So the knot of Eve's disobedience was loosed through the obedience of Mary; for what Eve, a virgin, bound by her unbelief, that Mary, a virgin unloosed by her faith. Death by Eve, life by Mary.'"[147]

---

[145] Ware, p. 264.
[146] "The Virgin," 7:316. *Complete Works of William Wordsworth* (Boston, Massachusetts: Houghton Mifflin, 1911).
[147] Ware, p. 263.

CHAPTER V

The belief never really surfaced until the twelfth century, when it was introduced as a feast in France. While it is certainly true that some Orthodox held to the belief, it is also true that great doctors of the Western church, led by St. Bernard of Clairvaux, "strongly objected, occasioning a controversy that divided Catholic scholars for about four centuries. The majority, including St.Thomas Aquinas, St. Albert and St. Bonaventure, opposed the doctrine implied in the feast, arguing that since Christ was the redeemer of all, and hence of Mary, all must have previously sinned (*cf.* Rom. v), including Mary,"[148] thus declaring that "in every natural conception the stain of original sin is transmitted and that, as Mary was conceived in a natural way, she was not exempt from this law."[149] In this they were confessing the traditional teaching of the church, which they shared with their Orthodox brethren. Various local bishops forbade the celebration of its feast.[150]

Some 650 years later, Pope Pius IX on December 8, 1854, declared the Immaculate Conception to be a dogmatic belief of the Church.

---

[148] *Encyclopaedia Britannica,* 1972, vol. 11, p. 1105.

[149] *The Oxford Dictionary of The Christian Church,* 3rd edition (Oxford: Oxford University Press, 1997), p. 821.

[150] Geoffrey Grigson & Charles Harvard Gibbs-Smith (eds.), *Ideas* (New York, New York: Hawthorne Books), p. 200.

FREQUENTLY ASKED QUESTIONS FROM ROMAN CATHOLICS

WHY DOES THE ORTHODOX CHURCH GIVE COMMUNION TO INFANTS?

In communing infants, the Orthodox Church is continuing a tradition of the early Christian Church that Rome also practiced until the twelfth century. In fact, in the Western church, "Communion was given to infants and young children after Baptism under the form of wine."[151] By the twelfth century the Western church started to discontinue the practice of giving communion under both species (bread and wine), giving only the communion wafer instead. Since wine was no longer given to the laity, this of course precluded communing very young infants, thus "baptismal Communion went out of use by the 12th century."[152]

The Orthodox Church continues the ancient practice of the Church in giving communion to infants, including those just baptized, thus following Christ's command, "Suffer the little children to come unto me, and forbid them not; of such is the kingdom of God" (Mark 10:14).

---

[151] Joseph Jungman, S.J., *The Mass of the Roman Rite, Its Origins and Development* (Westminster, Maryland: Christian Classics, 1992), vol. 2, p. 385.

[152] Ibid.

CHAPTER V

WHY DOES THE ORTHODOX CHURCH USE LEAVENED BREAD?

Here again, in her use of leavened bread the Orthodox Church is continuing a tradition of the early Church that Rome also practiced for the first 800 years. In talking about Western liturgical practices, Father Joseph A. Jungman, S.J., observes that there "...was the change which took place about this time in the type of bread used, the change to unleavened bread. Alcuin and his pupil Rabanus Maurus are the first indisputable witnesses to this new practice, which spread only very slowly."[153] Within a few hundred years the Orthodox were called heretics by their Western brethren for their continued use of leavened bread.

WHY DOES THE ORTHODOX CHURCH ALLOW A MARRIED PRIESTHOOD?

In the Orthodox Church as in the early Church, especially in the East, a married priesthood was the norm. At the First Council of Nicea (325) while debating a canon for enforced celibacy, St. Paphnutius of Egypt, blind in one eye and crippled from torture during the persecution (kissed by the Emperor Constantine in a touching scene during

---

[153] Ibid., vol. 1, p. 84.

FREQUENTLY ASKED QUESTIONS FROM
ROMAN CATHOLICS

the Council),[154] spoke against clerical celibacy, forcefully stating "Too heavy a yoke ought not to be laid upon the clergy"[155] and thus "prevented the canon, though he would have permitted a canon forbidding those who were ordained when unmarried to marry after ordination."[156]

A married clergy continued to be defended by local synods and ecumenical councils, ending with its explicit defense in canon 3 of the Sixth Ecumenical Council: "If anyone shall have dared, contrary to the Apostolic Canons, to deprive any of those who are in holy orders, presbyter or deacon, subdeacon of cohabitation and intercourse with his lawful wife, let him be deposed."[157]

The current position of the Orthodox Church on married clergy still reflects the tradition of the early Eastern Church:

> Orthodox priests are divided into two distinct groups, the 'white' or married clergy, and the 'black' or monastic. Ordinands must make up their mind before ordination to which group they wish to

---

[154] Leo Donald Davis, S.J., *The First Seven Ecumenical Councils* (Collegeville, Minnesota: The Liturgical Press, 1990), p. 58.

[155] *Encyclopaedia Britannica,* 1972, vol. 6, p. 634.

[156] Ibid., p. 634.

[157] Aristeides Papadakis, *The Christian East and the Rise of the Papacy*, (Crestwood, New York: St. Vladimir's Seminary Press, 1994), pp. 37-38.

CHAPTER V

belong, for it is a strict rule that no one can marry after he has been ordained to a Major Order. Those who wish to marry must therefore do so before they are made deacon. Those who do not wish to marry are normally expected to become monks prior to their ordination; but in the Orthodox Church today there are now a number of celibate clergy who have not taken their monastic vows. These celibate priests, however, cannot afterwards change their minds and decide to get married. If a priest's wife dies, he cannot marry again.[158]

The Western attitude to married clergy is reflected in the papal reforms of 1046-1073. Professor Colin Morris comments: "...the papal reform movement did not mark the abandonment of the monastic approach so much as its adoption as the policy of the Roman Church. One of the fundamental aims was to separate the clergy from the rest of society...."[159] Professor Aristeides Papadakis concurs: "Behind the campaign for celibacy, in sum, aside from the moral and canonical issues involved, was the desire to set all churchmen apart from and above the laity; the need to create a spiritual elite by the separation of the priest from the ordinary layman was an urgent priority."[160]

---

[158] Ware, p. 298.
[159] Colin Morris, *The Papal Monarchy–The Western Church from 1050 to 1250* (Oxford, England: Clarendon Press, 1989), p. 99.
[160] Papadakis, p. 37.

FREQUENTLY ASKED QUESTIONS FROM ROMAN CATHOLICS

One of the things that struck me when I entered the Orthodox Church from Roman Catholicism was the absence of that "gulf" that separates a celibate clergy from the laity. A married priesthood creates a definite psychological bond between the laity and their priests.

The enforcement of priestly celibacy was only achieved in the West through stiff, even violent opposition, as Professor Morris relates: "...there were riots in synods when bishops attempted to issue regulations separating priests from their wives. The reforming Archbishop John of Rouen was driven with stones out of his diocesan synod in 1072, exclaiming, 'O God, the heathen are come into your inheritance!' and in 1074 there were angry scenes in various parts of Europe, including Paris, where the clergy condemned the reforming decrees as 'intolerable and therefore unreasonable.' It became standard in papal decrees to refer to the women of priests, whether married or not, as concubines, and eventually the Roman Church gave force of law to the denial of the validity of the marriage of priests."[161]

---

[161] Morris, p. 104.

CHAPTER VI

Frequently Asked Questions from Protestants

WHERE DO YOU FELLOWSHIP?

The above question has been directed at me many times by Protestant acquaintances and speaks volumes about their view of church service, lacking as it does any sacramental mystery. For the Orthodox Christian, "Liturgical services are not one of the 'aspects' of the Church; they express its very essence, are its breath, its heart-beat, its constant self-revelation. Through the sacraments and especially through the sacrament of the Holy Eucharist, the Church, as one theologian worded it, always 'becomes that which it is,' i.e., the Body of Christ."[162]

Orthodox Christians along with their Roman Catholic brethren enjoy a shared history and a common sacramental tradition, which places their

---

[162] Alexander Schmemann, *Liturgy and Life: Christian Development through Liturgical Experience* (New York, NY: Department of Religious Education, Orthodox Church in America, 1993), pp. 12-13.

questions in a more readily understood framework. Protestantism, however, is the result of a 16th century revolt against medieval Roman Catholicism, which, while rejecting its worst excesses, also jettisoned much of the genuine catholic tradition of the Church. The questions, while drawn from a variety of Protestant denominations, reflect much of that lost tradition.

WHY DOESN'T THE ORTHODOX CHURCH ACCEPT THE BIBLE AS THE SOLE RULE OF FAITH? WHY INCLUDE ALL THOSE MAN-MADE TRADITIONS?

The Orthodox Church has always declared and professed that the Bible is the inspired word of God. The Bible forms the cornerstone of her tradition, for the "Church recognizes one and only one source of authority for her faith and practice: the apostolic tradition. The Divine Scriptures are part–albeit the most important part–of that tradition. To set Scriptures up as something over and apart from tradition is to have the tail wagging the dog."[163] It is a teaching of the Orthodox Church that Sacred Scripture and Tradition are inextricably intertwined and it is this bond that preserves its unity of doctrine.

---

[163] Clark Carlton, *The Way* (Salisbury, Massachusetts: Regina Orthodox Press, 1997), pp. 135-136.

FREQUENTLY ASKED QUESTIONS FROM PROTESTANTS

Protestant objections to tradition are appealed to in the following verses: "...you have made void the commandment of God for your tradition. Hypocrites, well hath Isaias prophesied of you saying: *This people honoureth me with their lips: but their heart is far from me. And in vain do they worship me, teaching doctrines and commandments of men*" (Matt 15: 6-9). "Beware lest any man cheat you by philosophy, and vain deceit; according to the tradition of men, according to the elements of the world, and not according to Christ" (Col 2:8). What is being condemned here. however, is not tradition per se, but false human traditions that run counter to sacred teaching.

There is a great oral tradition that the Church has preserved and uses in her capacity as the teacher of Scripture. For the Apostle John ends his Gospel by reminding us that "there are also many other things which Jesus did; which, if they were written every one, the world itself, I think, would not be able to contain the books that should be written" (Jn. 21:25). An example of this oral tradition of the teachings of Christ that are not to be found in the Gospels is discovered in Acts 20:35: "I have shewed you all things, how that so labouring you ought to support the weak, and to remember the word of the Lord Jesus, how he said: It is a more blessed thing to give, rather than to receive." Here

St. Paul is passing on an oral tradition of Christ's teaching that he himself did not hear preached.

Again in 1 Peter 3:19-20 we learn, "In which also coming he (Christ) preached to those spirits that were in prison: (the realm of the dead) Which had been some time incredulous, when they waited for the patience of God in the days of Noe, when the ark was a building: wherein a few, that is, eight souls, were saved by water." Here we learn by oral tradition–for it is nowhere to be found in the Gospels–that Christ "descended to the dead."   A further example of this kind of oral tradition is preserved in Jude 1:9: "When Michael the archangel, disputing with the devil, contended about the body of Moses, he durst not bring against him the judgment of railing speech, but said: The Lord command thee." This incident is not to be found in the Old Testament or in the Gospels, but is known only through oral tradition.

St. Paul exhorts us to "stand fast; and hold the traditions which you have learned, whether by word or by our epistle" (2 Thes 2:14). This oral teaching is evident when we read: "Faith then cometh by hearing; and hearing by the word of Christ" (Rom 10:17). For the early Christians, in the absence of any New Testament literature, an oral tradition was all they had, as had the people of the Old Testament before them. For much of the Old

FREQUENTLY ASKED QUESTIONS FROM PROTESTANTS

Testament existed for hundreds of years as an oral tradition before it was written down.

An Orthodox Christian would turn the question around and ask their Protestant brethren on what basis do they accept the Bible as the *sole rule of faith?* Certainly not from the Bible itself, for no such claim is to be found in its pages. Even the much quoted passage they use to support the *sole rule of faith* argument from 2 Tim 3:17: "All scripture, inspired of God, is profitable to teach, to reprove, to correct, to instruct in justice" contradicts the very case they are trying to make, as John Henry Newman points out:

> It is quite evident that this passage furnishes no argument whatever that the Sacred Scripture, without Tradition, is the *sole rule of faith;* for, although Sacred Scripture is *profitable* for these four ends, still it is not said to be *sufficient.* The Apostle requires the aid of Tradition (2 Thess.2:15). Moreover, the Apostle here refers to the Scriptures which Timothy was taught in his infancy. Now a good part of the New Testament was not written in his boyhood: some of the Catholic Epistles were not written even when St. Paul wrote this, and none of the Books of the New Testament were then placed on the canon of the Scripture books. He refers, then, to the Scriptures of the Old Testament, and if the argument from this passage proved anything, it would prove too much, viz., that the Scriptures of

123

the New Testament were not necessary for a rule of faith.[164]

A further argument against the Bible as the *sole rule of faith* is that universal literacy is a fairly recent achievement–it was only by 1910 that it was largely eliminated in most countries of Western Europe.[165] In pre-Renaissance Europe the vast majority of people were illiterate. In fact, it has been estimated that even by the late Tudor and early Stuart periods–approximately a hundred years after the Protestant Revolt–two-thirds of the people of England were illiterate.[166] Therefore, to imagine that ploughmen and shepherds in the country read the New Testament, or that blacksmiths and carpenters in towns pored over its pages in the corner of their masters' workshops is pure fantasy–the Bible as the *sole rule of faith* was definitely not for them.

No book can guarantee its own inspired status: only an outside authoritative body can do that. Numerous books claim to be inspired, e.g., the Book of Mormon and the Koran; however, the mere claim of these books itself is insufficient proof.

---

[164] John Henry Newman, *On Biblical Inspiration and Infallibility* (Oxford, Oxford University Press, 1979), p. 131.

[165] *Encyclopaedia Britannica,* 1972, vol. 11, p. 1088.

[166] Christopher Hibbert, *The English: A Social History 1066 –1945* (New York: W.W. Norton & Company, 1987), p. 270.

FREQUENTLY ASKED QUESTIONS FROM PROTESTANTS

When it comes to the Bible, it is the Church and only the Church that guarantees its inspired status, since it existed before the writing of the New Testament, i.e., the New Testament is the product of the Church; the Church is not the product of the New Testament. Therefore, the Church rightly claims that she is the mother of the New Testament. While Roman Catholics would understand the claim, Protestants would probably consider it blasphemous. However, the fact is that the Church existed long before any of the documents that now comprise what we call the New Testament. Furthermore, none of them was written with the idea that they would one day be placed together with the Old Testament to create what we now call "The Bible." St. Paul, for instance, would have been shocked to see his thirteen letters written to various Christian communities declared to be inspired scripture.

Due to the sheer volume of literature in circulation (much of it being apocryphal or heretical) that appeared within two hundred years after Christ's death, the Church was compelled to make a choice in order to preserve its doctrine. For instance, there was the *Gospel of Peter*, tainted with the heresy of Docetism, that enjoyed enormous popularity with a number of churches, the *Gospel of Nicodemus* with its story of Christ's trial, the *Gospel of Mary (Magdalene)*, and even a

Gospel of Judas (Iscariot). Also, there were numerous Acts according to Andrew, Barnabas, Bartholomew, Matthew, Paul, Peter, Philip, Thaddaeus, and Thomas. The list is long, with much of it displaying a naïve, unrestrained imagination.

As mentioned before, no book can guarantee its own inspired status; only an outside authoritative body can do that. With her God-given authority, this is what the Church did: after sifting through vast quantities of literature and many debates, she declared the twenty-seven books of the New Testament to be inspired. Their canonical status was ratified at a series of synods at Hippo Regius in 393 and at Carthage in 397 and 419. The formation of the canon of the New Testament was formally closed for East and West at the Trullan Council in Constantinople (692).[167]

WHY DOES THE ORTHODOX CHURCH INSIST ON CALLING MARY THE MOTHER OF GOD (THEOTOKOS)?

Protestant reaction to this ancient title by which the Church addresses Mary runs from a self-conscious uneasy acceptance to outright denial–"how could God possibly have a mother?" The

---

[167] *Encyclopaedia Britannica*, 1978, vol. 3, p. 578

question really centers not on Mary, but on Christ Himself and our understanding of the Incarnation. Their respective responses clearly demonstrate a graded scale within the Protestant community, from superficial to outright Nestorianism. This was one of the principal heresies within the Church and was named after Nestorius, Patriarch of Constantinople (d. c. 451), who denied that there are two distinct natures, divine and human, united in the person of Christ (hypostatic union). Thus like some of his latter-day Protestant fellow travelers, he could just bring himself to acknowledge that Mary was only the mother of Christ's human nature, hence denying Mary the title *Theotokos* (God-bearer).

For this the Council of Ephesus (431) formally condemned and anathematized him: "...to Nestorius the new Judas: Know that for thy impious doctrines thou wast deposed by the holy synod agreeably to the laws of the Church...."[168] When most people who object to Mary's title think it through, they can readily see that Christ's human and divine nature cannot be separated. Thus in honoring Mary as "the Mother of God," the Church preserves and safeguards the doctrine of the Incarnation.

---

[168] Mansi, IV, 1227.

CHAPTER VI

HOW DOES THE ORTHODOX CHURCH DEFEND THE PERPETUAL VIRGINITY OF MARY?

It was the Arian heretic Helvidius, a contemporary of St. Jerome, who first impugned Mary's perpetual virginity by claiming that "brethren" of the Lord referred to the natural brothers and sisters of Jesus who were born to Mary and Joseph following His birth. However, St. Jerome, in his work *De perpetua virginitate Beatae Mariae adversus Helvidium,* displays his gift of invective and biting wit in demolishing Helvidius' "novel, wicked" ideas and "daring affront to the faith of the whole world," a sample of which follows:

> We have played the rhetorician and have carried ourselves somewhat after the manner of platform orators. But it was you, Helvidius, who made us do it; for though the gospel shines today in fullest splendor you would have it that virgins and married women share equal glory. And since I know that you, having been bested by the truth, will resort to disparagement of my life and to bad-mouthing my character--little ladies generally act in this fashion; and, when their masters have bested them, they sit in the corner and wish them evil--I can only tell you in advance that your railings will rebound to my glory, when you lacerate me with the same mouth you used in your detraction of Mary. The Lord's

servant and the Lord's Mother will have an equal portion of your canine eloquence.[169]

The scriptural verses that Helvidius and many Protestants focus on are as follows: "As yet he was speaking to the multitudes, behold his mother and his brethren stood without, seeking to speak to him" (Matt. 12:46). "Is not this the carpenter, the son of Mary, the brother of James, and Joseph, and Jude, and Simon? Are not also his sisters here with us?" (Mark 6:3). "Have we not the power to carry about a woman, a sister, as well as the rest of the apostles, and the brethren of the Lord and Cephas?" (1 Cor. 9:5).

The term "brethren of the Lord", as St. Jerome points out, does not necessarily infer a first blood relationship. Because the Semitic language lacked a word that described "cousin," the word *Achim,* "brethren," had a very wide meaning indeed, from the identification of genuine brothers and sisters to cousins and stretching to members of the same tribe. Thus we are told that Lot was Abraham's brother, when in fact he was Abraham's nephew (Gen. 14:14). In Genesis 29:15 Jacob is described as the brother of his uncle Laban. On many occasions the term "brethren" could be used to

---

[169] As quoted from William A. Jurgens, *The Faith of the Early Fathers* (Collegeville, Minnesota: The Liturgical Press, 1970), vol. 2, p. 191.

describe people not related by blood or by tribe as in Jer. 34:9, Dt. 23:7 and Esd. 5:7.

Nowhere in the New Testament do we find any of the "brethren" explicitly referred to as Mary's son or sons–a systematic omission that carries the implication that Jesus was indeed her only son. Furthermore, Jesus is always referred to as "the son of Mary" as we saw in Matt 12:46, not "a son of Mary."

At His crucifixion, we see that Jesus commended His mother to the care and protection of His beloved disciple John: "When Jesus therefore had seen his mother and the disciple standing whom he loved, he saith to his mother: Woman, behold thy son. After that, he saith to the disciple: Behold thy mother. And from that hour, the disciple took her to his own" (Jn. 19:26-27). If Jesus had other "brethren," this entrustment of their mother to someone outside the clannish Jewish family would have been an unbelievable, incomprehensible act of effrontery.

Furthermore, Helvidius, like many Protestants since him, latched on to the passage from Matt 1:25 as proof that, following the birth of Christ, Mary must have had other children because "...he knew her not till she brought forth her firstborn son."

FREQUENTLY ASKED QUESTIONS FROM PROTESTANTS

St. Jerome cites by numerous examples that St. Matthew's use of the word "until" was purely idiomatic, i.e., a form of expression peculiar to the Hebrew people that only referred to what is done, without any regard to the future. Thus, in Genesis 8:6-7 we read that "Noe, opening the window of the ark which he had made, sent forth a raven, which went forth and did not return, **till** the waters were dried up upon the earth." That is, did not return at all. God said to His Divine Son: "sit on my right hand **until** I make thy enemies thy footstool." Is Christ to sit at God's right no longer after His enemies are vanquished?

Also in I Maccabees 5:54 we learn that "...they went up to mount Sion with joy and gladness, and offered holocausts, because not one of them was slain, **till** they had returned in peace." That is, not one was slain before or after they had returned. In Deuteronomy 34:6 we are told that Moses was buried in "the valley of the land of Moab over against Phogor: and no man hath known of his sepulchre **until** this present day." The problem, of course, is that we still don't know! Many more examples could be given to show that the word "until" does not disprove Mary's perpetual virginity.

St. Jerome also proves by his scriptural examples that an only-begotten son was also called firstborn or first-begotten, because

CHAPTER VI

according to the Law the firstborn males were to be consecrated to God: "Sanctify unto me every firstborn that openeth the womb among the children of Israel..." (Ex.13:2).

WHY DOES THE ORTHODOX CHURCH BAPTIZE INFANTS?

Some Protestants say that in the New Testament converts were required to believe and be baptized, which is why only adult baptism is recorded. But obviously, when a new religion is first taught, it must be addressed to adults and they must be asked to believe in the new religion before submitting to its requirements. But nowhere in the New Testament is there the faintest suggestion that only adults could be baptized.

Christ expressly said, "Amen, amen, I say to thee, unless a man be born again of water and the Holy Ghost, he cannot enter into the kingdom of God" (John 3:5). Here the universal necessity of baptism is stressed, which must include children since they are also to be natural heirs of His kingdom: "Suffer the little children, and forbid them not to come to me: for the kingdom of heaven is for such" (Matt. 19:14). Christ also sent the Apostles to teach and baptize all nations (Matt. 28:19) and the term "all nations" certainly includes men, women, and children. Our Lord did not say, "baptize only the adults of all nations." We are told more than once in the New Testament that when adults were converted, they and all their household were baptized–"all their household" must have included infants and young children.

St. Paul tells us that baptism for Christians replaces circumcision (Col. 2:11-12) and under the Mosaic Law, we know that it was mainly infants who were circumcised and thus aggregated to God's chosen people. Is the New Law to be less perfect than the Old? Is Christ unable to save any except adults?

The witness of the early Church to the practice of infant baptism is solid, as the following small sampling testifies:

> The Church received from the Apostles the tradition of giving Baptism even to infants. For the Apostles, to whom were committed the secrets of divine mysteries, knew that there is in everyone the innate stains of sin, which must be washed away through water and the Spirit. Origen, *Commentaries On Romans*, 5,9. (post A.D. 244)

> As to what pertains to the case of infants: you said that they ought not to be baptized within the second or third day after their birth, and that the old law of circumcision must be taken into consideration, and

that you did not think that one should be baptized and sanctified within the eighth day after his birth. In our council it seemed to us far otherwise. No one agreed to the course that you thought should be taken. Rather, we all judged that the mercy and the grace of God ought to be denied to no man. St. Cyprian of Carthage, *Letter of Cyprian and of his Colleagues in Council to the Number of Sixty-Six: To Fidus,* 64 (59), 2, (A.D. 251-252).

Do you have an infant child? Allow sin no opportunity; rather, let the infant be sanctified (39) from childhood. From his most tender age let him be consecrated by the Spirit. St. Gregory Nazianzus, *Oration On Holy Baptism,* 40,17, (A.D. 381).

The custom of Mother Church (22) in baptizing infants is certainly not to be scorned, nor is it to be regarded in any way as superfluous, nor is it to be believed that its tradition is anything except Apostolic. St. Augustine, *The Literal Interpretation of Genesis,* 10, 23,39, (inter A.D. 401-415).

The Orthodox Church has always taught that, when it comes to baptizing children, the belief of the parents in Christ is sufficient, just as it is sufficient in the natural life that parents believe on their child's behalf that instruction is necessary and give it, and that parents believe that sound morals are necessary and teach the good principles that flow from them. They don't wait for the child to make up his own mind on all these things.

Later, the child will know and accept for himself
the wisdom of these things. In the same way,
parents who know that Christ is the way, the truth,
and the life choose Christ on their child's behalf.
They set their child, who is a continuation of their
own life, upon the right path by teaching him or her
about Christ. At the earliest possible moment, they
secure the implantation of the life of Christ in the
child's soul by baptism. Later on, the child gladly
accepts and ratifies this gift, as he grows into an
understanding of the faith and begins to live
consciously according to its precepts.

WHAT DOES THE ORTHODOX CHURCH TEACH REGARDING GUARANTEED SALVATION?

The Orthodox Church's objection to the doctrine
of guaranteed salvation is firmly based in Scripture
and Tradition, which radically oppose it. The New
Testament, while preaching the mercy and love of
God and His desire for the salvation of all, is also
full of warnings to those who might presume His
mercy and grow lax in their faith, as St. Paul warns
the Philippians: "Wherefore, my dearly beloved, (as
you have always obeyed, not as in my presence
only, but much more in my absence,) with fear and
trembling work out your salvation" (Philippians
2:12). This great apostle even tells the Corinthians

that the salvation he constantly preaches could be lost for himself: "But I chastise my body, and bring it into subjection, lest perhaps, when I have preached to others, I myself should become a castaway" (1 Cor 9:27).

To those who believe that a "born again" experience and the acceptance of Christ as their "personal Savior" assures them of salvation, Christ declares, "Not every one that saith to me, Lord, Lord, shall enter the kingdom of heaven" (Matt 7:21). St. Paul solemnly reminds them: "For we must all be manifested before the judgment seat of Christ, that every one may receive the proper things of the body, according as he hath done, whether it be good or evil" (2 Cor 2:10).

Our one single act of faith will not shield the deeds and acts of a lifetime, as God "will render to every man according to his works" (Rom 2:6). For those Christians living devout lives, St. Paul warns them to continue in their lives of sanctity, lest they lose their salvation. "See then the goodness and the severity of God: towards them indeed that are fallen, the severity; but towards thee, the goodness of God, if thou abide in goodness, otherwise thou also shalt be cut off" (Rom 11:22).

Statements such as these completely undercut the doctrine of assured salvation, a doctrine almost unknown for the first 1,500 years until the Protestant Revolt. In keeping with the teaching of the New Testament and the Patristic Tradition, the Orthodox Church has constantly taught that salvation is a lifelong process where Christians are "saved daily through repentance and the yielding of their mind, heart and will to God."[170] St. Paul likened it to a race for an "incorruptible crown" where "they look forward to their glorification with Jesus at the Second Coming" (1 Cor 9:25).

WHAT DOES THE ORTHODOX CHURCH TEACH REGARDING SALVATION OUTSIDE THE CHURCH?

The Orthodox Church has always confronted the world as the Church of Jesus Christ. Christ did not found many churches–He only founded one. She is the Church of the Apostles and Martyrs and of the Seven Ecumenical Councils that has an unbroken line back to the apostles. This claim flows from her sense of unity with God and God's bond with His Church. As the Orthodox theologian Alexis Khomiakov explains it in his essay, "The

---

[170] Anthony M. Coniaris, *Introducing the Orthodox Church* (Minneapolis, Minnesota: Light and Life Publishing Company, 1982), p. 48.

Church is one. Its unity follows of necessity from the unity of God."[171]

Since God and His Church cannot be separated, the Orthodox Church teaches that there is no salvation outside the Church. However, this does not mean that all those souls outside the Church are damned, any more than all those souls within the Church are saved. As Augustine observed, "How many sheep there are without, how many wolves within!"[172] God does not demand the impossible; those people who genuinely try to obey their consciences and/or have been denied the knowledge that Christ is the Savior of mankind may merit eternal salvation. Plus, there are people who are not visibly members of the Church but whose membership is known only to God. However, if anyone is saved, he must, in some sense, be a member of the Church, but in what sense, it is not always possible to say.

Alexis Khomiakov explains the Orthodox position very succinctly:

Inasmuch as the earthly and visible Church is not the fullness and completeness of the whole Church which the Lord has appointed to appear at the final

[171] *The Church Is One,* section 1, as quoted in Timothy Ware, *The Orthodox Church* (Harmondsworth, England: Penguin Books, 1973), p. 249.
[172] *Homilies on John,* xiv, 12.

judgment of all creation, she acts and knows only within her own limits; and …does not judge the rest of mankind, and only looks upon those as excluded, that is to say, not belonging to her, who exclude themselves. The rest of mankind, whether alien from the Church, or united to her by ties which God has not willed to reveal to her, she leaves to the judgment of the great day (*The Church Is One,* Part 2).[173]

THE VENERATION OF SAINTS' RELICS IS VERY DIFFICULT FOR ME TO ACCEPT. COULD YOU PLEASE COMMENT.

What most Protestants object to is the conveying of supernatural grace to inanimate physical matter, e.g., holy water, medals, oil, candles, etc. At the top of the list of this objectionable practice stands the veneration of saints' relics, which to many of them smacks of the occult.

In fact, this practice is embedded in both Scripture and Tradition. The Orthodox Church does not hold that relics of themselves possess any innate magical quality. But God Himself can certainly grant favors through the relics of saints, thus honoring His saints and rewarding the faith

---

[173] As quoted in Timothy Ware, p. 316.

and piety of some given Christian. St. Matthew tells us that when the diseased came to Christ "they besought him that they might touch but the hem of his garment. And as many touched, were made whole" (Matt 14:36).

Again we read of a woman who touched the hem of Christ's garment and was cured: "And immediately Jesus knowing in himself the virtue that had proceeded from him, turning to the multitude, said: who hath touched my garments?" (Mark 5:30). In the Acts of the Apostles we find that "God wrought by the hand of Paul more than common miracles. So that even there were brought from his body to the sick, handkerchiefs and aprons, and the diseases departed from them, and the wicked spirits went out of them" (Acts 19:11-12).

These practices were not only confined to the New Testament, for when we read Kings 13:21-22 in the King James Bible we find that a dead man who was being buried in the sepulchre of Elisha was restored to life the moment his body came into contact with the bones of the great prophet of God.

We see this teaching preserved in the early Church following the martyrdom of St. Polycarp (A.D. 155-157):

FREQUENTLY ASKED QUESTIONS FROM PROTESTANTS

He therefore (the Evil One) proceeded to do his best to arrange that at least we should not get possession of his mortal remains, although numbers of us were anxious to do this and to claim our share in the hallowed relics.... So that after all, we did gather up his bones–more precious to us than jewels, and finer than pure gold–and we laid them to rest in a spot suitable for that purpose. [174]

This great tradition of the Church, with its proper understanding of sacred objects and relics in Christian worship, was enshrined by the Second Council of Nicea (787). These included "candles and incense...the form of the life-giving cross...the holy Gospel Book, and to other sacred objects, even as was the pious custom in ancient days also."[175]

WHAT DOES DEIFICATION MEAN?

Many people when they hear the term "deification" immediately think of some "New Age" movement. However, for the Orthodox Christian it means to become partakers of the divine nature– not to become God, which would not only be blasphemous heresy, but impossible.

---

[174] *Early Christian Writings,* translated by Maxwell Stanforth (London, England: Penguin Classics, 1987), pp. 130-131.

[175] John Julius Norwich, *Byzantium—The Early Centuries,* (London: Viking, 1988), p. 371.

CHAPTER VI

Deification in the Orthodox sense means that we are to become God-like by virtue of His grace or divine energies, not His essence, which would be impossible. "Historically, deification has often been illustrated by the 'sword and fire' example. A steel sword is thrust into a hot fire until the sword takes on a red glow. The energy of the fire interpenetrates the sword. The sword never becomes fire, but it picks up the properties of fire."[176] It is in this way that "our humanity is interpenetrated with the energies of God."[177]

This teaching of deification has a solid Scriptural base: "As all things of his divine power which appertain to life and godliness...that by these you may be made partakers of the divine nature" (2 Peter 1:3-4). When the Jews accused Jesus of blasphemy he quoted the passage from (Psalm 82:6) "Is it not written in your law: *I said you are gods*?" (John 10:34).

That we are to become partakers of the divine nature is the dominant theme of St. John's Gospel and the Pauline Epistles. This, therefore, "is the final goal at which every Christian must aim: to become god, to attain *theosis*, 'deification' or

---

[176] *The Orthodox Study Bible* (Nashville, Tennessee: Thomas Nelson Publishers, 1993), p. 561.
[177] Ibid.

'divinization.' For Orthodoxy, man's salvation and redemption mean his deification."[178]

---

[178] Ware, p. 236.

The Orthodox Church Comes to North America

And how shall they preach unless they be sent, as it is written: How beautiful are the feet of them that preach the gospel of peace, of them that bring glad tidings of good things!

Faith then cometh by hearing; and hearing by the word of Christ. Romans 10: 14,15,17.

In the vast stretches of Eastern Siberia lies the region of Irkutsk, an area of rolling hills and broad valleys, covered by dense taiga, coniferous forest, and containing the largest freshwater lake in the world–Lake Baikal. Its claim as the world's largest lake is not due to its size (12,000 square miles) but to its volume, i.e., at 5,250 feet deep in most places, it has the same volume of water as the Baltic Sea, or as much as the five Great Lakes of North America combined.

In the long bone-chilling winters when the temperature drops to –50 to –60 Fahrenheit, the condensation is suspended in the air in the form of ice crystals and the frozen sap in the trees snaps like rifle shots. Even in the hottest summers the

CHAPTER VII

soil remains frozen two feet below the surface. It was in this environment that John Veniaminov (St. Innocent) was born on August 26, 1797, in the small village of Anginskoe, a settlement of small, low, timber houses, huddled together for fear of loneliness in the vast Siberian landscape, with many of them displaying those typically Russian carved window frames painted in a variety of colors.

It was here in eastern Siberia that St. Innocent spent the formative years of his life, thus preparing him for the rigors and hardships of an Alaskan mission from which men would shrink. At the tender age of nine, he was enrolled at the Irkutsk Theological Seminary, where during his eleven-year stay his intellectual brilliance brought him to be ranked as the seminary's top student.

In addition to his seminary studies, St. Innocent's vast intellectual curiosity led him not only to read every book in the library dealing with history and science, but also to learn how to make clocks and musical instruments. To these skills he added furniture making, carpentry, and blacksmithing.

John married and in 1821 was ordained to the priesthood, serving in the church in Irkutsk. In 1823, the Holy Synod requested the Bishop of Irkutsk to provide a missionary priest to work among the native people of Alaska. The entire clergy of Irkutsk, including Father John, refused to volunteer for such a task. However, Father John had a change of heart and accepted the appointment. When he told his wife of his decision, the poor horror-stricken woman burst into tears. Had she known what lay ahead, she undoubtedly would have wailed louder and longer.

Father John began his journey on May 7, 1823, accompanied by his wife, his young son Innocent, his mother-in-law, and his brother Stephen. The first 2,000 miles were covered by barge on the Lena River, where they disembarked at the small town of Yakutsk. From there they set out on horseback, journeying 1,000 miles through mosquito-infested marsh (Siberian mosquitoes are legendary), and where blackflies are capable of drawing blood, to the little port of Okhotsk on the Pacific coast of Siberia.

On July 29, 1824, Father John arrived at Unalaska, an island near the end of the 1,500 mile-long chain of cold, moisture-sodden islands that divide the North Pacific from the Bering Sea. He quickly set to work building a church with his own hands, which he completed in a little over a year. Preaching to the natives entailed a great deal of long-distance travelling by dog sled and by kayak in rough icy seas. The intense cold of the ocean

CHAPTER VII

easily penetrated the thin-skinned kayak, causing his legs to freeze, which resulted in permanent damage from arthritis and rheumatism.

Being a gifted linguist, he learned the language of the Aleuts and wrote the first book of grammar for them. He then translated the Divine Liturgy, the Gospel of St. Matthew and other sacred church books into their own language. During Father John's sojourn in Unalaska, he wrote one of the most outstanding, critically acclaimed works in Russian geographical and ethnological literature; the three-volume *Notes on the Islands of the Unalaska Division.* After ten years, he was transferred to the busy port town of New Archangel (Sitka), Russia's New World capital where he was to remain for five years.

While on a trip to Russia in order to gain much-needed help and supplies for his mission, Father John learned of his wife's death. After a period of grieving for the woman who had shared in his labor and hardships, and settling his six children in suitable schools, Father John was tonsured a monk, taking the name Innocent. Shortly after, Tsar Nicholas appointed him as Bishop of Alaska. For the next ten years he labored hard, preaching the Gospel from one end of this huge diocese to the other. In 1850 he was elevated to the rank of archbishop and given even more territory for which to care.

THE ORTHODOX CHURCH COMES TO NORTH AMERICA

In 1867 he had the shock of his life when he received the news of his election as Metropolitan of Moscow. The humility of the man was revealed by his response, "Who am I to take the word and power of my predecessors?"[179] On Holy Saturday, 1879, at the age of eighty-one, almost blind, in constant pain and worn out from his fifty-eight years of labor, he died. His final words were, "Do not allow any speeches at my burial; there is too much praise in these. Instead, preach a sermon over me, for this can give instruction to people."[180] This giant of the Church, St. Innocent, Metropolitan of Moscow, Apostle to America, after fifty-eight years of hard labor had laid a solid foundation of Orthodoxy in the New World for others to follow and enlarge.

Some thirty years prior to the arrival of St. Innocent, St. Herman of Alaska arrived on Kodiak Island with a team of missionary monks from the famous Valaam Monastery, in Russian Finland. These missionary monks were hindered in their work by being seriously underfunded and by constantly having to defend the native Aleuts from the exploitative, rough Russian fur traders.

---

[179] Paul D. Garrett, *St. Innocent, Apostle to America* (Crestwood, N.Y.: St. Vladimir's Seminary Press, 1979), p. 293.
[180] Ibid., p. 318.

CHAPTER VII

To avoid the continuous confrontation with the fur traders, St. Herman moved to Spruce Island, his "New Valaam," sometime between 1808 and1818 to live, pray in solitude, and teach and care for his Aleuts. The children adored this gentle mystic, calling him "Apa" (grandpa).

The Russian people have always revered a *staretz* (holy man), like Father Zossima whom Dostoevsky immortalized in *The Brothers Karamazov,* and, as the ancient chronicles describe them, who "bore upon themselves the humiliation of Christ, not having a city here, but seeking a future one." Thus it was that one day a group of Russian naval officers sought out this solitary *staretz* who slept on a bare board and was gifted with prophetic insight. St. Herman loved to talk and as he sat in the midst of these naval officers, he asked them what it was they most wanted in life. The usual answers came back -- wealth, position, a beautiful wife, etc. After St. Herman's probing questions, they all agreed that only God was worthy of their true love and commitment. "Then" said St. Herman, "from this day, from this hour, from this moment, let us love God above all and do His will!"

In 1837 St. Herman died peacefully among his beloved Aleuts, who grieved the loss of their gentle "Apa." In the forty-three years St. Herman spent among the Aleuts of Alaska, he was always a gentle, caring, inspiring witness of Christ, exhibiting the very best of the Orthodox monastic tradition: "If any man will follow me, let him deny himself, take up his cross, and follow me" (Mk 8:34). While he was taken from the people who loved him, not everything was lost, for the value remained. To this day his memory is cherished among the native people of Alaska.

After the United States' purchase of Alaska in 1867, the episcopal see was transferred to San Francisco five years later. Thus far, the Orthodox Church's bridgehead in North America was limited to Alaska and the Pacific coast. However, within eight years a dramatic change was to take place that would see this thin, Orthodox bridgehead expand to embrace the length and breadth of North America. Beginning in the 1880's an enormous Slavic immigration began, cresting forty years later in the early 1920's. The first great wave was composed of Uniats, consisting of Galicians and Carpatho-Russians from Austro-Hungary. These Uniats were former Orthodox Christians who had been united with Rome since 1596 at the Treaty of Brest Litovsk.

It was from the ranks of these Uniat immigrants that a leader emerged, named Father Alexis Toth, who in 1891 initiated a return to the Orthodox Church. By the early 1900's, 225,000 former

CHAPTER VII

Uniats had returned home to the Church of their ancestors. Russians, Ukrainians, Greeks, Syrians, Rumanians, Serbians, and Albanians followed this first wave. Today there are well over five million Orthodox Christians in North America.

Prior to 1917, the Orthodox Church in North America came under the canonical jurisdiction of the Russian church, with all the bishops being sent from Russia. One of them was the future Patriarch Tikhon of Moscow, who served as Archbishop of North America for nine years (1898-1907). However, following the Russian Revolution of 1917, the situation in the North American Church under Russian leadership became confused and disordered. The result was that the Orthodox Church dissolved into separate jurisdictions based on national origin.

Even though they are now under separate jurisdictions, the North American Orthodox Christians are united in doctrine, liturgical life, and canon law. Blessed with a strong, common liturgical integrity, there is a sense of unity among these more than five million Orthodox Christians in North America. It is expected that the Orthodox Church in North America will one day be united again into a single autocephalous church (appointing its own head, i.e., independent) with its own metropolitan or patriarch.

THE ORTHODOX CHURCH COMES TO NORTH AMERICA

Orthodox Christians both in the United States and Canada have built some of the most beautiful churches and spared no expense on magnificent interior decoration. The vast majority of these churches have large parish halls that are used for social activities. Because they appear so ethnically homogeneous and self-contained, they have been dubbed "ethnic clubs." This, of course, was a predictable development, especially when we reflect on the obvious linguistic and cultural differences these people had to overcome. My family and I were received into the Orthodox Church in just such a church in Vancouver, British Columbia. A number of very old Russians who had fled the Revolution have been members of the parish for over seventy years. Their courteous, courtly Old World manners never fail to charm. This Russian church could not have been more gracious, kind, and welcoming–we are, by the way, not the only English-speaking converts.

Many of the Orthodox Churches are beginning to reach out into the community with a good number of dioceses establishing mission churches. They are also introducing more English into the Liturgy–our Russian church is now about fifty percent English.

To Glimpse the Soul of a Nation

So that we ourselves also glory in you in the churches of God, for your patience and faith, and in all your persecutions and tribulations, which you endure. 2 Thessalonians. 1:4

In June, 1997, my wife and I, accompanied by our two youngest children, had an opportunity to visit Russia. It was interesting to glimpse, even briefly, the soul of an Orthodox country emerging from seventy years of brutal atheistic oppression. Near the end of our visit, I was standing on the steps of the Pushkin Museum in Moscow gazing in wonderment at the rebuilding of the Church of Christ the Savior.

Work began on the original church in 1839 and involved some of Russia's best architects, artists, and craftsmen; it was consecrated in the presence of Tsar Alexander III on May 26, 1883, having taken forty-four years to complete. This massive, majestic, cruciform basilica church, built in thanksgiving for Russia's victory over Napoleon, cost over 15 million rubles, which was raised entirely by public donation.

CHAPTER VIII

This huge dazzling white church, clad with sheets of Podolian marble and Finnish granite, which should more properly be described as a cathedral, became one of the great architectural masterpieces of 19th century Moscow. Covering an area of 8,020 square yards, this 335-foot high church was crowned with five gilded domes–the main dome having a diameter of 100 feet. The belfry housed the largest bells in Russia.[181]

Renowned artists of the day had covered the inside walls of the church with murals, and 422 kilograms of pure gold was lavished on interior gilding. This grand vision was bathed in the warm glow of 3,700 candles. The November 1914 issue of *The National Geographic* in describing the interior wrote that "the effects obtained by the blending of red, white, gray marbles with gold quite beggar description." They went on to say that the Church of Christ the Savior will prove to be "one of the memories which every visitor will always cherish."[182]

On July 18, 1931, "*Pravda* announced that a committee headed by V. Molotov had decided to build a 'Palace of the Soviets' beside the Moscow River." Five months later this architectural masterpiece of the Church of Christ the Savior was

---

[181] Suzanne Massie, *Land of the Firebird* (London: Hamish Hamilton, 1980), pp. 387-388.

[182] As quoted by Suzanne Massie, p. 388.

dynamited on Stalin's orders. The marble, murals and chandeliers were used to grace the Moscow subway. In 1933 Stalin "commissioned a design by Yofon and Shchusev which envisaged an edifice 415 metres high, and six times more capacious than the Empire State Building. It was to be surmounted by a figure of Lenin three times taller than the Statue of Liberty, with an index finger 6 meters long."[183] Mercifully, this monstrosity was never built and thirty years later, Nikita Krushchev ordered that the crater be turned into a swimming pool.

Now an exact copy of the original church is being built on the same site, like a phoenix rising from the ashes. With its gilded domes blazing in the blue Moscow sky and its white marble facing, this majestic church (a three-ton gilt cross 30 feet high and 20 feet across adorns the main dome) presents a shimmering embodiment of the soul of the Orthodox Church that can triumph over incredible suffering and persecution.

The repression of Christianity in Russia under Soviet rule, outside that of the Roman persecution, is without parallel in history--for it was unrelenting, exacting, comprehensive, and systematic in its bold attempt to eliminate Christianity within its borders. During the first several decades of Communist rule, over 90,000 churches were

---

[183] Norman Davies, *Europe* (London, England: Pimlico, 1997), p. 747.

dynamited or bolted shut and left to rot. Some 7,000 were allowed to remain as housing, workshops, warehouses or even as swimming pools; the more famous churches and monasteries were turned into museums.

A particularly poignant moment for me was our visit to the beautiful Monastery of St. Cyril of the White Lake at Kirillov, near the town of Goritsky. As we drove through the town of Kirillov with its log houses and ample vegetable gardens and approached the great monastery, I recalled reading the account of Alexander Asimov. He was an art restoration expert, sent out to this monastery by the Soviet Government in the autumn of 1918 to take stock of its religious antiquities. During his stay, Asimov witnessed with considerable distress the Communist terror directed against the Church. He describes the fate of the monastery's bishop and others:

This Saturday Bishop Varsonofy was arrested as he was coming back from Goritsky in the same carriage as myself.

At dawn the following day he was taken out into a field together with the Mother Superior of the Ferapontov Convent, two townspeople and two peasants; they were all shot dead....The shots were

TO GLIMPSE THE SOUL OF A NATION

fired from the back.... Staying here, far from pleasant, is now a real nightmare.[184]

The "nightmare" continued for the next 70 years in which 200,000 priests, monks, nuns and lay people were killed, tortured, or died in concentration camps. This "nightmare" ultimately engulfed Alexander Asimov himself, when he was executed in 1937.

Today signs of the Church's revival are very evident. Churches and monasteries all over Russia are being returned to the Church and over 50,000,000 people have officially rejoined the Orthodox faith. As welcome as this obviously is, it presents the Orthodox Church with a daunting, Herculean task of repairing, restoring, and staffing thousands of buildings and properly catechizing an avalanche of people–all this with severely depleted coffers and clergy. They desperately need our prayers and help.

On a visit to the lovely provincial city of Yaroslavl, we were informed that the nearby convent now has 127 nuns–many of them being young women from the four corners of Russia. During our time in Yaroslavl, we visited the beautiful 17th century Church of St. Elijah the Prophet, with its five green cupolas representing

---

[184] From letter dated September 4, 1918, from art restoration expert Alexander Asimov to renowned art specialist Igor Grabar.

CHAPTER VIII

Christ and the four evangelists. Catherine the Great was so impressed with this church that she ordered the surrounding buildings to be demolished, thus creating a large square that offered an unobstructed view of this fine structure. However, in 1937, the Soviet Government ordered the church to be blown up. The people of Yaroslavl journeyed to Moscow with various noted artists and academics to plead for its survival. The Communist Government eventually relented, but in an act of spite they bolted the church shut–"we will spare your church but you are not going to use it."[185] People were then concerned about the fate of the beautiful 17th century frescoes, painted by renowned artists. How long would they last in damp unheated conditions?

The prayers of the people must have been heard, because during the Second World War the Russian Army used the church to store their felt boots, which were apparently stacked to the roof, thus creating a perfect antidote for the damp conditions. The beautiful frescoes survived. As we entered the church, half a dozen young art restoration experts were examining the frescoes. There is a great deal of this sort of activity across Russia as she attempts to repair 70 years of ruinous neglect.

---

[185] As quoted to the author by the tour guide in Yaroslavl.

TO GLIMPSE THE SOUL OF A NATION

A tremendous emotion was visible when the Divine Liturgy was celebrated in that church for the first time since the Communist Revolution, for there were a number of ninety-year-old people in attendance who had not been in the church for 70 years.

Before we left the Church of St. Elijah the Prophet, four young men chanted some sacred music of the Russian Orthodox Church. This turned out to be one of the memorable moments of our visit. These four young men had beautiful voices, which the acoustics of this 17th century church seemed to lift and amplify, giving an incredible dynamic range to their voices, to the point that they seemed like a full choir. The sheer tonal quality was astonishing–the church was filled with the sound of a glorious, haunting, spiritual longing. As I listened, I cast my eyes around at the icons and the frescoes and understood more clearly why the faith of this people could never be crushed. Some of the tourists were visibly moved, to the point of having tears in their eyes.

On our last day in Moscow, which was a Sunday, we attended the Divine Liturgy at the Novodevichy Convent. This huge convent was built as a fortress at the bend of the Moskva River in the 16th century and played an important part in the city's struggle against the Tartar and Polish invaders. In the 16th and 17th centuries the convent entered a period of high privilege, for it was here that women from royal and aristocratic families took the veil. It was at this convent that Peter the Great confined his sister Princess Sofia Alexeyvna for 15 years, following her abortive coup to unseat him.

Entering one of the churches on the convent grounds, we found a young priest in the corner of the narthex hearing confessions, while gathered in front of him was a tightly packed crowd of about 60 people patiently waiting their turn. There was also a good number of young men and women in the congregation. The spiritual beauty of the Liturgy combined with the deep emotional quality of the choir, so typically Russian, was very striking. There was a great deal of reverence among the people as they stood throughout the Liturgy, constantly crossing themselves during the litanies (prayers of supplication), while making frequent hand prostrations during other parts of the service.

Two radically opposing views dominate human life–the spiritual and the material, and it is ironic that it was in Russia for the first time that the materialistic view sought to eliminate the spiritual. For Russian people, more than most, are profoundly moved by beauty, whether it is in poetry, art, music, the glory of nature or the innocence of a child. There is even a word in their vocabulary that expresses the experience of the soul when it is stirred by its encounter with beauty; it is the word *umilenie*. It means to experience a multitude of emotions, e.g., tenderness, pity, and rapture almost to the point of tears. To the Russian, possessing an inability to respond to beauty with *umilenie* is to pass through this life in darkness.

Seventy years of dialectical materialism has produced little in art and architecture that is worth seeing. Much of the architecture is relentlessly drab or even slightly sinister, such as the seven skyscrapers that dot the Moscow skyline, which are disdainfully referred to as "Stalinist Gothic"– buildings more reminiscent of "Gotham City." It is ironic that what the Soviet Government so tirelessly worked to destroy is precisely what most visitors wish to see. When people visit Russia, it is her spiritual achievements that are most sought after and admired, e.g., the beautiful churches, monasteries, and the icons–that sacred art form which so well reflects the deepest feelings of the Russian people. When I looked again at the rebuilding of the Church of Christ the Savior and reflected on all I had seen in Russia, I felt I was witnessing the stirring of a nation's soul.

CHAPTER IX

On Being Orthodox

The greatest misery of man is neither poverty nor sickness nor misfortune in life, nor the disappointments of the heart nor death; it is the misery of not knowing why he is born, suffers and dies.[186]

Orthodoxy is a lived faith, with morning and evening prayers and a rich calendar of saints' feast days and fasts that are woven like a tapestry throughout the year. In his book *The Waters of Marah,* P. Hammond relates the central role the liturgical calendar has in the lives of Orthodox Christians:

Nobody who has lived and worshipped amongst Greek Christians for any length of time but has sensed in some measure the extraordinary hold which the recurring cycle of the Church's liturgy has upon the piety of the common people. Nobody who has kept the Great Lent with the Greek Church, who has shared in the fast which lies heavy upon the whole nation for forty days, who has stood for long hours, one of an innumerable multitude who crowd the tiny Byzantine churches of Athens and

---

[186] As quoted by Anthony Coniaris in *Eastern Orthodoxy: A Way of Life* (Minneapolis, Minnesota: Light and Life Publishing, 1966), p. 5.

overflow into the streets, while the familiar pattern of God's saving economy towards man is represented in psalm and prophecy, in lections from the Gospel, and the matchless poetry of the canons; who has known the desolation of the holy and great Friday, when every bell in Greece tolls its lament and the body of the Savior lies shrouded in flowers in all the village churches throughout the land; who has been present at the kindling of the new fire and tasted of the joy of a world released from the bondage of sin and death–none can have lived through all this and not have realized that for the Greek Christian the Gospel is inseparably linked with the liturgy that is unfolded week by week in his parish church. Not among the Greeks only but throughout Orthodox Christendom the liturgy has remained at the very heart of the Church's life.[187]

It is without question that the Orthodox Church is the only one that maintains the great feasts of Christianity in the life of her faithful. It is the richness of this lived tradition that will sustain Orthodox Christians in this intensely secular society, as it has in other difficult periods. This is a truth voiced by Thomas Smith when he wrote:

> Next to the miraculous and gracious providence of God, I ascribe the preservation of Christianity among them to the strict and religious observation of the Festivals and Fasts of the Church....This certainly is the chiefest preservative of Religion in

---

[187] Hammond, pp. 51-52.

those Eastern countries against the poison of Mahometan superstition. For Children and those of the most ordinary capacities know the meaning of those holy Solemnities, at which times they flock to the Church in great companies, and thereby retain the memory of our blessed Savior's Birth, dying upon the cross, Resurrection, and Ascension, and keep up the constant profession of their acknowledgement of the necessary and fundamental points of Faith, as of the doctrine of the Blessed Trinity, and the like. And while they celebrate the sufferings and martyrdoms of the Apostles of our Lord and Savior Jesus Christ, and other great saints, who laid down their lives most joyfully for His name, and underwent with unwearied and invincible patience all the Torments and Cruelties of their Heathen Persecutors, they take courage from such glorious examples, and are better enabled to endure with less trouble and regret the miseries and hardships they daily struggle with.[188]

The Church Year begins on September 1st and is dominated by the Twelve Great Feasts, excluding Pascha (Easter), which being the Great Feast of Feasts stands alone in its magnificence.

---

[188] "An Account of the Greek Church" as quoted in Anthony Coniaris, *Introducing the Orthodox Church* (Minneapolis, Minnesota: Light and Life Publishing Company, 1982), pp. 18-19.

CHAPTER IX

THE TWELVE GREAT FEASTS

The Nativity of the Most Holy Theotokos
(Sept. 8th)

It is entirely fitting that the First Great Feast in the Church's calendar should celebrate with great joy the birth of the Mother of God:

Thy Birth, O Mother of God and Virgin, brought tidings of joy to the whole universe: for the Sun of Justice, Christ our God, has shone forth from Thee... *Troparion of the Feast (Tone 4).*

By choosing the Nativity of the Most Holy Theotokos as the First Great Feast on the Church calendar, we are presented with a picture of human holiness that is **more honorable than the cherubim and more glorious than the seraphim**. Mary, the Mother of God, the great and merciful Intercessor, holds a very special position in the hearts of Orthodox Christians, as the New Eve whose docile obedience to the will of God opened the doors of Paradise for fallen humanity.

The Exaltation (or Raising Up) of the Life-Creating Cross
(Sept. 14th)

This feast has its origins in Jerusalem, when the Emperor Constantine dedicated the Basilica of the Resurrection erected by him in 335. With the discovery of the True Cross by the Emperor's mother St. Helena, the Feast for the Dedication of the Basilica was replaced with the Feast of the Exaltation of the Life-Creating Cross.

This great Feast of the Church, in glorifying the Raising of the True Cross, reminds us that Christ's crucifixion was the culmination of our salvation:

Who his own self bore our sins in his body upon the tree: that we, being dead to sins, should live to justice: by whose stripes you were healed (2 Peter 2:24). We should therefore rejoice because **...the curse was abolished, incorruptible life flowed again, earthly creatures have acquired deification and the demon has been decisively overthrown** (*Vespers, Stichera of Tone 5*).

The Entrance of the Theotokos into the Temple
(Nov. 21st)

This Feast falls shortly after the commencement of the Nativity Fast (Advent). It finds its origins in the early traditions of Palestinian Christians, who relate that in the fourth century St. Helena built a

church there in honor of the Entrance of the
Theotokos into the Temple.

Here we see the righteous Joachim and Anna,
bringing Mary (as a young child) to live a
consecrated life in the Temple. In this consecrated
life, lived in union with God, detached from the
world and its cares, we are given an example of
how we should lead our spiritual lives.

**Today is the prelude of the good will of God,
of the preaching of the salvation of mankind.
The Virgin appears in the Temple of God, in
anticipation proclaiming Christ to all. Let us
rejoice and sing to her: Rejoice, O divine
Fulfillment of the Creator's dispensation!**
Troparion of the Feast (Tone 4)

The Nativity of Christ
(Dec. 25th)

St. Gregory of Nyssa wrote in 380 that the
Christians of Cappadocia (modern-day Turkey)
celebrated this great Feast on December 25th,
rather than January 6th, while Rome had been
celebrating it on this day since 354. This date was
set 9 months after the date of Christ's conception
(the Annunciation), which was placed on the date
of His crucifixion in the year A.D. 33. December

25th coincided with the pagan celebration of the birth of the unconquered sun (*natalis solis invicti*).

Our Savior, the Dayspring from the East, has visited us from on high: And we who were in darkness and shadow have found the Truth. For the Lord is born of the Virgin. (*Exapostilarion*)

The Baptism of Christ in the Jordan (Epiphany)
(Jan. 6th)

Here we find one of the oldest Feasts in the Christian Church, the others being Pascha (Easter) and Pentecost. This Epiphany (manifestation) commemorates the manifestation of Christ, first to the Magi and then of His divinity at His baptism in the Jordan River.

Today Thou hast appeared to the universe, and Thy light, O Lord, has shone on us, who with understanding praise Thee: Thou hast come and revealed Thyself, O Light Unapproachable. *Kontakion of the Feast (Tone 4)*

CHAPTER IX

The Presentation of Our Lord in the Temple
(Feb. 2nd)

This Feast represents the crossroads between the "Old Testament and the New. St. Simeon symbolizes the departing Old Testament, exemplified by men of righteousness and prophets who in spite of all their doubts and searchings entertained the firmest belief in what had been foretold of the promised salvation. The righteous Simeon **took Him up in his arms** and the Old and New Testaments stood together: the Old, departing, held in his arms and blessed the New. This was unity and continuity, a direct link and a development; the Law and the promised manifestation of the Grace of God as His Only Begotten-Son, the Redeemer."[189]

By thy Nativity, Thou didst sanctify the Virgin's womb and didst bless Simeon's hands, O Christ God. Now Thou hast come and saved us through love. Grant peace to all Orthodox Christians, O only Lover of Man. *Kontakion of the Feast (Tone 1)*

---

[189]By a Monk of St. Tikhon's Monastery, *These Truths We Hold* (South Canaan, Pennsylvania: St. Tikhon's Seminary Press, 1992), pp. 170-171.

The Annunciation to the Most Holy Theotokos
(March 25th)

The announcement made by the angel Gabriel to the Virgin Mary (Luke 1:26-38), "the mystery which surpasses the limits of human reason is accomplished–the Incarnation of God" (Monk Gregory). The Gelasian and Gregorian sacramentaries, along with the acts of the Councils of Toledo (656) and Trullo (692), are the first authentic allusions we have to this Feast.[190]

Today is the beginning of our salvation, the revelation of the eternal mystery! The Son of God becomes the son of the Virgin as Gabriel announces the coming of Grace. Together with him let us cry to the Theotokos: Rejoice, O Full of Grace, the Lord is with you! *Troparion of the Feast (Tone 4)*

The Entrance of Our Lord into Jerusalem
(Palm Sunday, one week before Pascha--*a moveable feast.*)

Here the triumphant entrance of Christ into Jerusalem on His way to voluntary suffering and death is celebrated, fulfilling the prophecy:

---

[190] *Encyclopaedia Britannica*, 1972, vol. 1, p. 1012.

173

Rejoice greatly, O daughter of Sion, shout for joy, O daughter of Jerusalem: BEHOLD THY KING will come to thee, the just and savior: he is poor, and riding upon an ass, and upon a colt the foal of an ass. (Zech 9:9)

The Ascension of Our Lord Jesus Christ
(40 days after Pascha/Easter — *a moveable feast*)

This great Feast has been celebrated since the fourth century. In fact, St. Augustine was already claiming that in his day it was celebrated "in all the world." The Ascension celebrates the final redemptive act of Christ, i.e., birth, passion, death, and resurrection are now completed. He now opens for us the gates of Heaven:

And if I shall go, and prepare a place for you, I will come again, and take you to myself; that where I am, you also may be (John 14:3).

The Descent of the Holy Spirit (Pentecost)
(50 days after Pascha — *a moveable feast*)

"This descent of the Holy Spirit was the making of the new covenant by God with the new Israel—

the Church—whereby the grace of the law-giving Holy Spirit took the place of the law of Sinai."[191]

Blessed art Thou, O Christ our God, Who hast revealed the fishermen as most wise by sending down upon them the Holy Spirit; through them Thou didst draw the world into Thy net. O Lover of man, Glory to Thee! *Kontakion of the Feast (Tone 8)*

The Transfiguration of Our Lord and Savior Jesus Christ
(Aug. 6th)

The Transfiguration celebrates the revealing of the infinite glory of the Second Person of the Blessed Trinity. This Feast is believed to be of ancient origin, as excavations on Mount Tabor, the traditional site of the Transfiguration, have revealed the remains of a church, which seem to confirm the claim of the Early Church that St. Helena had dedicated a church there in 326.

On the mountain wast Thou transfigured, O Christ God, and Thy disciples beheld Thy glory as far as they could see it; so that when they

---

[191] Leonid Ouspensky and Vladimir Lossky, *The Meaning of Icons* (Crestwood, New York: St. Vladimir's Seminary Press, 1982), p. 199.

would behold Thee crucified, they would understand that Thy suffering was voluntary, and would proclaim to the world that Thou art truly the Radiance of the Father! *Kontakion of the Feast (Tone 7)*

The Falling Asleep of the Most Holy Theotokos (Dormition)
(Aug. 15th)

For the churches both East and West, this is the principal Feast of the Virgin Mary. Originating in the East, the feast came to Rome in the middle of the 7th century "under the name of the Falling Asleep of the Mother of God. At Rome the name 'Dormition' or 'Falling Asleep' gave way before long to the new title that was to prevail in the West: the 'Assumption,' which at first hardly meant more than death or passing, but in time came to imply a real resurrection."[192]

Neither the tomb, nor death, could hold the Theotokos, who is constant in prayer and our firm hope in her intercessions. For being the Mother of Life, she was translated to life by the One who dwelt in her virginal womb! *Kontakion of the Feast (Tone 2)*

---

[192] *Encyclopaedia Britannica,* 1972, vol. 2, p. 632.

Of the Twelve Great Feasts of the Orthodox Church, we see that three, being dependent on Pascha, are moveable, while the remaining nine are fixed. Eight of the Feasts celebrate Christ and four the Mother of God.

THE FEAST OF FEASTS – THE HOLY PASCHA OF THE LORD (EASTER)

Christ Is Risen!

The importance of this Feast that celebrates the resurrection of Christ is underscored because it is placed outside the Twelve Great Feasts in a class by itself. It is the principal Feast in the Orthodox Church Calendar–not Christmas, as in the West. "Its origins go back to the beginnings of Christianity and it is probably the oldest Christian observance of the kind after Sunday, which was regarded as the weekly celebration of the resurrection."[193]

It is interesting that in many languages the name for this Feast is derived from the Hebrew word *Pasch* or *Passover. Pascha* in Latin, *Paques* in French, *Pasg* in Welsh, *Pasen* in Dutch or Flemish. It is claimed by Bede that the English

---

[193] Ibid., vol. 7, p. 865.

word Easter is derived from *Eostre,* the name of a pagan Saxon goddess of Spring.

The Orthodox Church maintains the tradition of the Early Church, in that the resurrection of Christ is not only an annual celebration, but also dominates her liturgical and spiritual life throughout the year. Thus in her Divine Liturgy the Orthodox Church has retained the early Christian sense of rejoicing in Christ's victory over death and sin:

Thou didst descend into the tomb, O Immortal, Thou didst destroy the power of death. In victory didst Thou arise, O Christ our God, proclaiming 'Rejoice' to the myrrhbearing women, granting peace to Thy apostles, and bestowing resurrection on the fallen. (*Kontakion of the Feast (Tone 8)*

FASTING

Behold in the day of your fast your own will is found, and you exact of all your debtors. *Isaias 58:3*

During a church dedication ceremony in north Washington State, I fell into a conversation with a second generation Greek Orthodox American. When the discussion turned to fasting, he told me that his parents only fasted during the last week of Lent. Upon telling his mother that he and his wife

178

kept the traditional Lenten Fast, i.e., seven weeks without meat, fish, dairy products, eggs, wine and oil, his mother scornfully replied, "Fanatics!"

His mother, of course, missed the point, because fasting and asceticism aren't just for monks and "fanatics," they are key elements in the spiritual growth of all Christians. Self-control and self-denial are absolutely essential if we are to advance on the ascetic road of undistracted prayer that leads to union with God. For the "Orthodox Church, regarding man as a unity of soul and body, has always insisted that the body must be trained and disciplined as well as the soul. Fasting and self-control are the first virtue, the mother, root, source, and foundation of all good."[194] The four main fasts are as follows:

GREAT LENT –
    commences seven weeks before Pascha.

THE FAST OF THE APOSTLES –
    begins on the first Monday eight days
    following Pentecost, ending on the eve of the
    Feast of Saints Peter and Paul, June 28th.

THE DORMITION FAST –
    lasts two weeks from the 1st to August 14th.

---

[194] Ware, p. 306.

CHAPTER IX

THE NATIVITY FAST –
lasts forty days from November 15th to
December 24th.

The weekday Fasts are Wednesdays for the betrayal of Christ by Judas Iscariot and Fridays for the Crucifixion. Other fasting days are the Exaltation of the Life-Giving Cross, the Beheading of Saint John the Baptist, and the eve of Epiphany. As mentioned earlier, the fast means eliminating from the diet meat, fish, dairy products, eggs, wine, and oil.

These fasting traditions that instill so much vitality and vigor into Christian life date back to the Early Church. However, as with so many other traditions, the Orthodox Church is now the only church that maintains them. "Early in 1966 Pope Paul VI promulgated new laws for Roman Catholics....Fast days, which had included all the weekdays of Lent, the vigils of Pentecost, the Immaculate Conception and Christmas, and the Ember days were reduced to two, Ash Wednesday and Good Friday."[195] Furthermore, in North America, they eliminated the Friday Fast (the Wednesday Fast disappeared long ago) and reduced the fast before reception of the Eucharist from 12 hours to one.

---

[195] *Encyclopaedia Britannica*, 1972, vol. 9, p. 108.

CHAPTER X

The Challenge

The world is trying the experiment of attempting to form a civilized but non-Christian mentality. The experiment will fail, but we must be very patient in awaiting its collapse; meanwhile redeeming the time, so that the Faith may be preserved alive through the dark ages before us, to renew and rebuild civilization, and save the World from suicide. T. S. Eliot, *Thoughts after Lambeth*

Thirty years ago it was the hippie flower-children of Haight-Ashbury and Woodstock with their beads, head bands, and battered V.W. buses who formed the counter-culture. To the music of Simon and Garfunkel and the urgings of Timothy O'Leary ("Tune in, turn on, drop out"), they rejected society's materialistic culture and social mores. Today with the rapid decline of Christianity and the equally rapid retreat of its values from the legal system, public life, and social conventions of society, traditional Christians now find that they are the counter-culture. It is a post-Christian world in that, while it has lost the Gospel message, for Christians the Kingdom of Christ remains etched more sharply by the gathering darkness of moral decay.

CHAPTER X

The great challenge facing Orthodox Christians in this post-Christian pagan world is their spiritual survival and hence their eternal salvation. In this, they will only be successful if they cleave more closely to the Church who will nourish and sustain them, as she has nourished and sustained her flock in the past under the domination of Romans, Mongols, Arabs, Turks, and Communists— adversity is no stranger to the Orthodox Church. At the center of her enduring spirit is a divine flame that is unconquerable. "Behold I am with you all days, even to the consummation of the world" (Mark 28:20). This promise is reflected in one of the great lessons of history, i.e., the Church achieves her most brilliant image when she encounters the abrasive quality of evil, manifested in persecution, oppression, and tribulation.

The reality of life is spiritual; e.g., love, justice, charity, mercy, kindness, forgiveness, hatred, envy, jealousy, pride, etc., are not three-dimensional objects that you can see, touch, and feel–they are purely spiritual, transcendent, eternal and unchanging. They are only experienced by looking inwards into the human soul, not to the material world that surrounds us. They dominate and dictate the human condition. The great battlefield is the human heart, for it is here that we find the origins of great acts not only of love, self-sacrifice, and lives devoted to charity and service to the less fortunate, but also of persecution, concentration camps, and genocide. This is a truth that dawned on Alexander Solzhenitsyn in the Soviet Gulag:

> And it was only when I lay there on rotting prison straw that I sensed within myself the first stirrings of good. Gradually it was disclosed to me that the line separating good and evil passes not through states, nor between classes, nor between political parties either–but right through every human heart– and through all human hearts....[196]

We enter the third millennium as a post-Christian, de-moralized, pagan society. We have been described as a society of technological giants and moral pygmies. For while technology has dramatically elevated our standard of living, our moral decay is undermining all our achievements. It has been said "the past is a foreign country;" this is certainly true when we look back to an age of unlocked doors and trustworthy neighbors. By contrast, we are forced to live in a world of bolted doors, home security systems, surveillance cameras, and security lighting--where unescorted women, strolling in parks, are only to be found in Impressionist paintings.

---

[196] Alexander Solzenhytsin, *The Gulag Archipelago* (Boulder, Colorado: Westview Press, 1997), vol. 2, p. 615.

CHAPTER X

Because the new paganism is a malevolent spirit, deeply hostile to Christianity, the Orthodox Christian must therefore realize that this is spiritual warfare with a force that can only be resisted by a strong countervailing spirit firmly rooted in the teachings of the Church and in an intense devotional life. This is the only defense we have from being engulfed by it.

As we descend into this vortex, many churches are in a mad frenzy to be relevant to the pagan culture that surrounds them, as we saw in the first chapter. In fact, some churches such as the Episcopal Church imposed voluntary censorship on passages of Scripture that are deemed offensive by the homosexual community:

> On pp. 952, 953, 971, and 984 of the *1979 Book of Common Prayer,* one may note in the daily lectionary that Romans 1:26-27 and I Corinthians 6:9-11 are deliberately omitted from the *lectio continua,* so that Episcopalians would be spared hearing what God thinks of homosexual sin.[197]

The day is fast approaching when those Biblical passages will be banned as homophobic hate literature.

---

[197] Frank Schaeffer, *Letters to Father Aristotle* (Salisbury, Massachusetts: Regina Orthodox Press, 1995), p. 209.

THE CHALLENGE

If we are to live and survive as Orthodox Christians, keeping bright the light of Christ in this new "Dark Age," then it behooves us to analyze this new paganism[198] in order to appreciate the challenges it brings with it.

THE NEW PAGANISM

It is crucial to understand that the paganism of classical antiquity that society *came out of* into Christianity is substantially different from the new paganism that society is *sliding into* from Christianity. It was pagan Greece with its love of beauty, reason, moderation, and belief in the individual worth of man that molded the mind and spirit of Western man.

Art is always a true reflection of a nation's spirit, as John Ruskin wrote: "Great nations write their autobiographies in three manuscripts, the book of their deeds, the book of their words and the book of their art. Not one of these books can be understood unless we read the two others, but of the three the only trustworthy one is the last."

When we view the art of classical Greece, we immediately capture her spirit, from the quintessential Greek temple with its functional

---

[198] The inspiration for this came from *Essays of a Catholic* by Hilaire Belloc (Rockford, Illinois: Tan Books and Publishers, 1992).

elegance and purity of line, to the incomparable sculptures of Praxiteles. Artist Paul Klee observed that a peaceful world produces realistic art, a view entirely shared by American historian Edith Hamilton:

> Greek art is intellectual art, the art of men who were clear thinkers, and it is therefore plain art. Artists than whom the world has never seen greater, men endowed with the spirit's best gift, found their natural method of expression in the simplicity and clarity which are the endowment of the unclouded reason. 'Nothing in excess,' the Greek axiom of art, is the dictum of men who would brush aside all obscuring, entangling superfluity, and see clearly, plainly, unadorned, what they wished to express.[199]

Paganism of the classical world with its love of wisdom, reason, moderation, and unshakeable belief in the individual worth of man was to provide a firm foundation on which a Christian civilization could be built.

If art is a true reflection of a nation's spirit that mirrors its aspirations and imagination, then modern art will have a great deal to tell us about the new paganism. The face of atheism is evident in its cult of the irrational, resulting in the dissolution of the human form, distorted reality,

---

[199] Edith Hamilton, *The Greek Way* (New York, New York: The Modern Library, 1961), p. 66.

lack of standards, and the mania for iconoclasm. It is this culture that Malcolm Muggeridge dismisses as "nihilistic in purpose, ethically and spiritually vacuous and Gadarene in destination."[200] Of the necessity of standards Joseph Wood Krutch wrote:

> Standards are imaginary things, and yet it is extremely doubtful if man can live well, either spiritually or physically, without the belief that they are somehow real. Without them society lapses into anarchy and the individual becomes aware of an intolerable disharmony between himself and the universe. Instinctively and emotionally he is an ethical animal.[201]

The late English writer and commentator Malcolm Muggeridge once observed that "reality is the bane of comedians." As editor of the British humor magazine *Punch*, Muggeridge would meet once a week with the magazine's assistant editors and writers and survey the political and social scene in order to create satire. He lamented, however, to being constantly confronted with the "tragic dilemma of how to ridicule a world whose

---

[200] Malcolm Muggeridge's foreword to the American edition of *The Trousered Apes* (New Rochelle, N.Y., Arlington House, 1972).

[201] Joseph Wood Krutch, as quoted by Duncan Williams in *The Trousered Apes,* p. 114.

CHAPTER X

reality so often outdoes their wildest and most daring inventions."[202]

When we survey the current art scene with its lack of standards, we are faced with situations that would rival and surpass anything that the most gifted satirist could create. The sheer imbecility of the two following examples, along with the critics' cultivated irrationality and ponderous, solemn assurances of their artistic merit, almost offers them immunity from criticism. If you find these hard to believe, please bear in mind that not only have they been exhibited in major urban art galleries, drawing reviews from national daily newspapers, but, in the interest of taste, I have had to edit out one of the exhibits.

Consider the winner of Britain's premier modern art award, the Turner Prize, which awarded $30,070 to Damien Hirst for his creation of *Mother and Child Divided*. This rather poignant title refers to a bisected dead cow and her calf floating in separate tanks of green formaldehyde. Critics have praised Hirst's creation "for its presentation of death without disgust or emotion and some critics say it contains elements of the Madonna and Child. Others remain unconvinced."[203] In making the award, the jury called attention to his

---

[202] Malcolm Muggeridge, *Tread Softly for you Tread on my Jokes* (London and Glasgow: Fontana Books, 1972), p. 16.
[203] *The Globe and Mail,* November 29, 1995, p. C2.

188

THE CHALLENGE

'extraordinary' "works, which include pickling dead sheep and sharks and sticking freshly hatched butterflies on a surface of wet paint."[204] In a televised interview Damien Hirst said "that his next ambition was to find a way of allowing a dead animal to decay inside a case without producing an offensive smell. 'Decay is actually quite a beautiful thing,' he said."[205] Hirst's "artistic works" with dead and decomposing animals have been sold to discriminating collectors for up to $320,000.

Recently, the Art Gallery of Mississauga in Ontario, Canada, had an exhibition entitled *Loving the Alien.* The curator Stuart Reid describes the exhibition in his catalogue as "the new foreignness of organic form" which is derived "from retouched photos in the tabloids to the supposed enhancement of beauty with plastic surgery, to the heralded genetic cloning of domestic animals—the alien has been absorbed into the very fabric of our everyday life and into our bodies. *Loving the Alien* presents works which are not a paean to paradise lost, but instead embrace the artificial." *Globe & Mail* art critic Gary Michael Dault describes some of the works as follows: "Stephen Schofield's testicular earthenware eggs, in their cast scrotum-like sacs, hang forlorn and vulnerable from lengths of raw steel pipe that run like handrails through the gallery. Philip Grauer's funny and disturbing cast-

[204] *The Province*, November 30, 1995, A46.
[205] Ibid.

aluminum shapes, sparkling with their lacquered, rubbed, candy-coated, kustom-kar surfaces, like weird, industrial slugs and caterpillars, Grauer's objects are slightly sinister. Self-contained to the point of narcissism in their own slick, unenterable beauty, they languish about the gallery on rubber mats, perch on hardware-store garbage cans, are plopped into plastic buckets or ooze out of overturned wastebaskets."[206]

In spite of their somewhat eloquent efforts at imputing artistic merit to these fantastic creations, they cannot conceal the fact that the Emperor has no clothes. Rather, what is immediately apparent is the inherent anti-civilizing thrust, manifested by a pathological preoccupation with ugliness and the baser elements of life, combined with a clinical obsession for the bizarre.

On this subject, Professor Duncan Williams is worth quoting: "The frenzied attempts to create a new art-form every month, the compulsive hunt for novelty (not only in the arts but in almost every sphere of human activity), the almost simultaneous acceptance and rejection of the latest, most modish, experiment however perverse or abnormal it may be—all these are symptomatic of a dying man's feverish attempts to clutch on to a swiftly ebbing life."[207]   In his *First Anniversairie,* the

[206] *The Globe & Mail*, October 4, 1997, p. C15.
[207] Williams, p. 41.

THE CHALLENGE

English poet John Donne describes how society "sickens of the ensuing moral and social anarchy" that results when a society abandons God: "then inevitably, by degrees, does 'the world's whole frame' fall 'out of joynt'; until finally it seems that the world becomes so sick that 'a Hectique fever' hath got hold of the whole substance, not to be controlled."[208]

The great gift for the traditional Christian is that while they are in the world they are not of the world. They have the moral framework of a transcendent world. Thus, armed with this perspective, they have a detached view that sees through the madness to the fact that "the Emperor has no clothes."

Music is undoubtedly one of the more intrusive, spiritual art forms that transcends reason and communes with the soul, and it is here that the new paganism has its greatest number of devotees in the hundreds of millions of youth addicted to rock music. Good music expresses the soul's deepest longing, while sublimating and refining the passions to serve a higher ideal. It is this tension that provides music with its beauty and nobility. The raw, blatant paganism of rock music with its message of unbridled sexual license, rebellion, and anarchy is of course the antithesis of this and as such is destructive to the spiritual life of our youth.

---

[208] John Donne, *The First Anniversairie,* II. 237-246.

CHAPTER X

As Allan Bloom, a professor of social thought at the University of Chicago comments:

> But rock music has one appeal only, a barbaric appeal, to sexual desire—not love, not *eros,* but sexual desire undeveloped and untutored. It acknowledges the first emanations of children's emerging sensuality and addresses them seriously, eliciting them and legitimating them, not as little sprouts that must be carefully tended in order to grow into gorgeous flowers, but as the real thing. Rock gives children, on a silver platter, with all the public authority of the entertainment industry, everything their parents always used to tell them they had to wait for until they grew up and would understand later.... Never was there an art form directed so exclusively to children.[209]

The new paganism is deterministic, which the *Oxford Dictionary* defines as "the doctrine that all events, including human action, are determined by causes regarded as external to the will." In other words, our actions are not free but are determined by our environment, nurturing, genes, single-parent family, illegitimacy, etc. Thus all too often we see responsibility for criminal acts transferred from the individual to some external stimuli, e.g., social, economic conditions–"society failed him."

---

[209] Allan Bloom, *The Closing of the American Mind* (New York, New York: Simon & Schuster, 1987), pp. 73-74.

THE CHALLENGE

"An anecdote about two genetically identical twin sons of a violent, drunken father, with the same upbringing, poignantly sums up this whole matter.

QUESTION TO FIRST TWIN: 'Why are you a drunken criminal?'

ANSWER: 'With a father like mine, who wouldn't be?'

QUESTION TO SECOND TWIN: 'Why are you *not* a drunken criminal?'

ANSWER: 'With a father like mine, who would be?'

In the anecdote above, the first twin has a determinist view of the mind, the second twin the opposite."[210]

If our actions are not dependent on our free will, then it logically follows that there is no right or wrong. This, of course, not only undermines Christian doctrine, it undermines our judicial system:

---

[210] William D. Gairdner, *The Trouble With Canada* (Toronto, Ontario: Stoddart Publishing Co. Limited, 1990), pp. 338-339.

CHAPTER X

Because any society that intends to be moral (freedom is a necessary precondition for moral life) must make a fundamental decision to opt for free will in order to conduct its affairs.... Man has an innate capacity to negate, or refuse, whatever he *is* at any moment, and thus to constantly re-create himself through free choice. This is a humanistic view that rejects materialism and determinism by declaring that regardless of our circumstances, we can always say "no"; that the glory of human existence is based on this power, and theories that remove it remove also our essential humanity. Man is always free to negate whatever he is to choose a new beginning however humble, to escape past forces by an act of free will.[211]

It is this determinism of the new paganism that ushers in despair, moral decay, the age of the anti-hero and victims, rather than people who could shape their destinies and even their age. Fifty years ago, Hilaire Belloc in his work *Essays of A Catholic* warned us prophetically as to what the new paganism would bring:

But the New Paganism despises reason, and boasts that it is attacking beauty. It presents with pride music that is discordant, building that is repellant, pictures that are mere chaos, and it ridicules the logical process.... Men do not live long without gods; but when the gods of the New Paganism come they will not be merely false; they will be evil. One

---

[211] Ibid., pp. 31and 341.

THE CHALLENGE

might put it in a sentence, and say that the New Paganism, foolishly expecting satisfaction, will fall, before it knows where it is, into Satanism.[212]

Offering a similar prophecy is social historian Paul Johnson:

> The greatest event of recent times–that "God is Dead," that the belief in the Christian God is no longer tenable–is beginning to cast its first shadows over Europe. Among the advanced races, the decline and ultimately the collapse of the religious impulse would leave a huge vacuum. The history of modern times is in great part the history of how that vacuum has been filled. Nietzsche rightly perceived that the most likely candidate would be what he called the 'Will to Power,' which offered a far more comprehensive and in the end more plausible explanation of human behavior than either Marx or Freud. In place of religious belief, there would be secular ideology.... And, above all the Will to Power would produce a new kind of messiah, uninhibited by any religious sanctions whatever, and with an unappeasable appetite for controlling mankind. The end of the old order, with an unguided world adrift in a relativistic universe, was a summons to such gangster-statesmen to emerge. They were not slow to make their appearance.[213]

[212] Hilaire Belloc, *Essays of a Catholic* (Rockford Illinois: Tan Books and Publishers, 1992), p. 26.
[213] Johnson, p. 48.

195

CHAPTER X

AND THIS TOO SHALL PASS

The despair, emptiness, alienation, and spiritual sterility of our post-Christian society that we see recorded in our art clearly points to the fact that human beings are spiritual creatures. As Professor Williams comments, "A belief in God (as ultimate reference) results in an assumption that there exist ultimate moral, aesthetic and legal standards. Conversely, a lack of such belief eventually creates a society in which every individual becomes his own moralist, aesthete and lawmaker. The outcome of such supra-individualism is social and artistic anarchy, a state into which Western society and possibly mankind as a whole appears to be rushing... Much of contemporary despair springs from an absence of absolute standards and of any authority, sacred or secular, and herein lies the paradox. Man desires freedom to do as he wishes but, once such a state is attained, sickens of the ensuing moral and social anarchy."[214]

That human beings being spiritual creatures will ultimately "sicken of the ensuing moral decay" is our great source of hope. Besides, and more importantly, because of her divine mission, the Church in her two-thousand-year history has presided over the funerals of many civilizations and societies, friend and foe alike–the Communist empire of the Soviet Union being the most recent–

---

[214] Williams, pp. 68, 101.

and she will preside over the funeral of our Western materialistic society as well. After his conversion to Christianity, T.S. Eliot finds that the fragmentary can only have meaning in relation to the timeless, to the Word of Christ:

> We shall not cease from exploration
> And the end of all our exploring
> Will be to arrive where we started
> And know the place for the first time.

In this connection, it seems likely that the central insights of the Christian faith have emerged unscathed by the onslaught of twentieth century secular materialism, contrary to the assumptions of many humanists. Christianity in recognizing man's capacity for good and evil has always been pessimistic about his ability to create a kingdom of heaven on earth–an insight that continues to escape modern liberal humanists. In this it is no more Jeremiah than Pollyanna. "It has also been skeptical about the absolute value of reason; from St. Paul through St. Augustine to Pascal and T.S. Eliot, many great Christian minds have denied that unaided reason can sustain, or save, man. Again Christianity was at home in crisis and persecution, in the catacombs and in exile, long before it was at home in the great civilization it helped to build. It is optimistic humanism which has been undermined by the ferment and uncertainty of twentieth century thought."[215]

The great challenge of the Orthodox Church in Western society is to preserve and spread the light of the Gospel in the spreading darkness of the new paganism. To do this effectively, she must resolve the overlapping jurisdictions especially prevalent in North America and her ethnic churches must adopt the vernacular in their Liturgy. For the Orthodox Church to reach the society around her, this is crucial, because the full doctrine and theology of the Church is revealed in her magnificent Liturgy and hymns. This is why it has always been a great tradition of the Orthodox Church that her Liturgy be in the language of the people. Thus it is an absolute travesty to have this rich catechesis fall on the ears of our youth in a language that is unintelligible--the Church cannot afford any more "lost generations."

While we are already seeing more churches using English in the Liturgy, it is a process that should be accelerated if the Orthodox Church is to assume her divine mandate in presenting herself as the "Pearl of Great Price." In conclusion, I could do no better than once again to quote Professor Ernst Benz:

---

[215] C.B. Cox and A.E. Dyson (eds.), *Twentieth Century Mind* (New York: Oxford University Press, 1972), vol. 3, pp. xii-xiv.

THE CHALLENGE

But in the deepest sense the Orthodox Church itself–sprung from the mystery of the Incarnation and preserving that mystery in itself, sprouting in the wilderness as the Church of ascetics, ravaged by the sandstorms of persecution, harassed by enemies of the faith and hostile fellows of the same faith, parched by immeasurable suffering and by inner and outer temptations, but yet unconsumed; burning with the fire of the Holy Spirit, aglow with the love of God, irradiated by the nuptial joy of the heavenly feast, illumined by the all-transfiguring power of the resurrected Lord–the Orthodox Church itself is **The Burning Bush.**[216]

---

[216] Ernst Benz, *The Eastern Orthodox Church*, p. 218.

INDEX

INDEX

INDEX

INDEX

I

Iconostasis, 93
Immaculate Conception, 110, 111, 112, 180
Incarnation, 127
Indissolubility of marriage, 103, 106, 108
Indissoluble unions, 105
Indulgences, 73
Ineffabilis Deus, 110
Infant baptism, 133
Inquisition, 85
Irkutsk, 145, 146

J

Jacob, 129
Jefferson Lecture in the Humanities, 38
Jerusalem, 45, 46, 169
Jesus Christ, 27, 88, 113, 122, 127, 130, 131, 132, 135, 140
John of Rouen, Archbishop, 117
Johnson, Paul, 15, 18, 195
Joyce, James, 18
Jungman, S.J., Father Joseph A., 114

K

Kayseri, 60
Keating, Fr. John, 107
Keats, John, 42
Kennedy, Congressman Joseph P., 108, 109
Kennedy, Sheila Rauch, 108, 109
King James Bible, 140
Kirillov, 158
Klee, Paul, 186
Koran, The, 124
Krushchev, Nikita, 157
Krutch, Joseph Wood, 187

L

Laban, 129
Lactantius, 82
Leavened, 114
Leavened bread, 114
Lena River, 147
Lenten Fast, 179
Leviticus, Book of, 104
Libellus, 50
Limbo, 69
London, 63
Lot, 129
Louis Vll (1137-1180), 106

M

Magi, 171
Marx, Karl, 195
Mary as "The Mother of God", 127
Mass of the Roman Rite, 31
Mediterranean, 49
Meyendorff, Fr. John, 70, 72
Middle Ages, 81, 82, 98, 105
Moab, 131
Molotov, V., 156
More, Thomas, 75
Mormon, Book of, 124
Morris, Colin, 116, 117
Mosaic Law, 66, 133
Moscow, 155, 156, 157, 160, 161, 163
Moscow subway, 157
Moses, 101, 122, 131
Moskva River, 161
Mount Tabor, 175
Mt. Erciyes, 60
Muggeridge, Anne Roche, 28
Muggeridge, Malcolm, 187
Muslim Bulgars, 90

N

Napoleon, 155
Nashville, Tennessee, 39

INDEX

INDEX

INDEX

INDEX

V

Valaam Monastery, 149
Vancouver, British Columbia, 153
Varsonofy, Bishop, 158
Veniaminov, John
    Innocent, St., 146, 147, 148
Virgin Mary, 110, 111, 112, 126,
    128, 130
Vladimir of Kiev, Prince, 90

W

Ware, Bishop Kallistos, 44
Ware, Timothy, 90
Washington State, 178
Western Christianity, 19

Western Church, 66, 82
Western Europe, 103
Westminster Shorter Catechism, 85
White House, 99
William Clyde DeVane Lectures,
    37
William of Ockham (1300-1347),
    80
Williams, Duncan, 22, 190, 196
Wordsworth, William, 111
Wright, Frank Lloyd, 41

Y

Yakutsk, 147
Yale University, 37
Yaroslavl, 159

Other books from Regina Orthodox Press
THE FAITH
Understanding Orthodox Christianity, An Orthodox Catechism

By Clark Carlt

Editorial Committee: Metropolitan **ISAIAH** (GOA Denver) Archbishop **DMITRI** (OCA Dallas
Bishop **BASIL** (Antiochian Archdiocese Wichita)

"An indispensable guide!"

Archbishop DMITRI (OCA Dall

"The best-written Orthodox catechism ever."

Metropolitan ISAIAH (GOA Denv

"A joyous event in the life of the Church."

Bishop BASIL (Antiochian Archdiocese Wichi

THE FAITH is the best Orthodox catechism in the English language. It is also the most widely
used by English-speaking Orthodox all over the world. **THE FAITH** is a beautifully written boo
that fully answers the question, *"What is it you Orthodox believe?"*

THE FAITH includes: The foundation of Orthodox faith + The Holy Trinity + Creation +
The fall of mankind + The promised Messiah + The Incarnation + The teachings of Chri
+ The birth and mission of the Church + The structure of the Church + Holy Baptism +
The Holy Spirit + The Mystical Supper + The Church at prayer and fasting + The myster
of love + God and gender + Monasticism + The Lord's *return* + *more...*
$22.95 286 Pages ISBN 0-9649141-1-5

THE WAY
What Every Protestant Should Know About the Orthodox Church

By Clark Carlt

*"I recommend this book to seekers of truth, to Protestants or others trying to find their way to the Christi
faith of the Apostles. Those Orthodox who wish to fully understand our faith should also read this book.'*
Archbishop **DMIT**

*"I wish I had read this book twenty years ago! It would have saved me years of spiritual wondering and
brought me into the Orthodox church."*

Frank Schaef

THE WAY is the highly praised and best-selling sequel to "The Faith." In a clear, well-written style Carlto
introduces the Orthodox Church to the non-Orthodox in a way that has drawn many converts to the Church
and deepened the faith of countless others. This is a great book for group study and the companion to "The
Faith."

THE WAY includes: *Sola Scriptura, the Protestant mistake + Proof-texts and the real teaching
of the Church + The nature of tradition + The structure of worship in the Early church + The
Protestant Reformation in the light of the Orthodox Church + A personal conversion story -
from Southern Baptist to Orthodox and more...*
$22.95 222 Pages ISBN 0-9649141-2-3

Regina Orthodox Press
P.O. Box 5288, Salisbury, MA 01952
1-800-636-2470 Fax: 508-462-5079
www.reginaorthodoxpress.com